CQRS (Command Query Responsibility Segregation)

Dedicated to my father Rambalak Ray

Table of contents

Overview

Overview

The CQRS pattern has become quite well known in this theory of domain driven design. However there are still lot of misconception around this patterns especially when it comes to applying it in the real word software projects. Should you use it with event sourcing?
Should you always have separate databases for reads and writes? How to implement command handlers. Book will answer all these questions and more. Some of the major topics that we will cover includes

- Refactoring Towards Task-based Interface and a way from CRUD based thinking.
- Implementing command and query handler decorators
- Extracting a seperate data storage for reads
- Common best practices and misconceptions around CQRS

By the end of this book you will know everything needed to start implementing

CQRS patterns in your own projects, Before
beginning this you should be familiar with
Java programming language.

.

Module 1 : Introduction

Introduction

If you are familiar with domain driven design,
you most likely heard about CQRS which
stands for "Command Query Responsibility
Segregation" . In Fact this pattern has
 become almost as well known as the concept
of domain driven design itself. However there
are still lot of misconceptions around this
pattern especially when it comes to applying it
in the real word software projects. Should you
use it with event sourcing?
Should you always have separate databases
for reads and writes? Should you make the
synchronization between reads and writes
asynchronous and so on. This book will
answer all these questions and more.

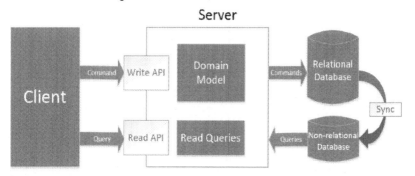

You will learn exactly what CQRS is? , the principles behind it and the benefits it can provide for your projects. You will also learn the common misconception and antipatterns around it. You will see at detailed step by step process of implementing this pattern in practice. The sample project will be working on is close to what you can see in the real world and i will explain each step on the way to CQRS in great details. Here is a quick outline of this book.

- Introduction
- Introducing a sample project
- Segregating Commands and Queries
- Refactoring Towards Task-based
- Interface
- Simplifying the Read Model
- Implementing CQRS
- Introducing a Separate Database for Queries
- Synchronizing the Commands and
- Queries Databases
- CQRS Best Practices and Misconceptions

In the 1st module we talk about what CQRS is, its origin and the benefits it can provide to your project. In the next module i will introduce an online student management system implemented without CQRS pattern in mind. You will first how the CRUD based API reduces the quality of ones code base and then much of user experience. In the 3rd module we will start the refactoring. We will segregate commands from queries by introducing two models as previously there was only one. You will see how it allow us to flood read operations from the domain model and thus make this model simpler. Nest you will learns what a CRUD based interface is and how to refactor it towards task based. In the 5th module we will simplify the read model. We will achieve that by passing the domain model and their ORM within data from the database. This will allow us to optimize the performance of reads in the application. In the next module we will look at implementing CQRS. In the 7th module we are going to introduce a seperate database for queries. And in module 8 implement synchronization between the two. Finally in the last module we talk about CQRS best practices and misconceptions. You will learn about common question that people will ask like the distinction from event sourcing. In this book you will see lot of refactoring techniques we shall explain in great detail as we go through them. For this book you will need a basic knowledge of Domain Driven Design.

CQRS and Its Origins

CQRS stands for Command-Query Responsibility Segregation. The idea behind this pattern is extremely simple. Instead of having one unified model, you need to introduce two: one for reads and the other one for writes, and that's basically it. Despite its simplicity, however, this simple guideline leads to some significant benefits. We will cover all of them in the subsequent modules. For now, let's elaborate on this basic idea, and talk about the origin of CQRS. CQRS was introduced by Greg Young back in 2010. Here's the book about CQRS he wrote in the same year. Greg, himself, based this idea on

the command-query separation principle
coined by Bertrand Meyer.

- Command
  - Produces side-effects
  - Returns void
- Query
  - Side-effect free
  - Returns non-void

Command-query separation principle, CQS for short, states that every method should either be a command that performs an action, or a query that returns data to the caller, but not both. In other words, asking a question should not change the answer. More formally, methods should return a value only if they are referentially transparent and don't incur any side effects, such as, for example, mutating the state of an object, changing a file in the file system, and so on. To follow this principle, you need to make sure that if a method changes some piece of state, this method should always be of type void, otherwise, it should return something. This allows you to increase the readability of your code base. Now you can tell the method's purpose just by looking at its signature. No need to dive into its implementation details. Note that it is not always possible to follow the command-query separation principle and there almost always will be situations where it would make more sense for a method to both have a side effect and return something.

CQS Limitations :

```
Stack stack = new Stack<String>();
stack.push("value"); // Command
String value = stack.pop(); // Both query and command
```

- When result of a query can become stale quickly

An example here is Stack. Its Pop method removes the element pushed into the stack last and returns it to the caller. This method violates the CQS principle, but at the same time, it doesn't make a lot of sense to separate those responsibilities into two different functions. Other examples include situations where the result of a query can become stale quickly, and so you have to join the query with the command. In this case, you both perform the operation and return the result of it.

Follows CQS :

```
public bool fileExists(String path){
        return file.exists(path);
}
public void writeToFile(String path, String content){
        if (!fileExists(path))
                throw new
        IllegalArgumentException();
        file.writeAllText(path, content);
}
```

Doesn't follow CQS :

```
public Result writeToFile(String path, String content){
        try{
                file.writeAllText(path, content);
                return Result.ok();
        }
        catch (fileNotFoundException e){
                return Result.fail("File not found");
        }
}
```

For example, here, on the top, you can see two methods, one for writing to a file, and the other one for ensuring that this file exists. The idea here is that before calling this method, the client code needs to make sure the file exists by using this one. The FileExists method is a query here. It returns a Boolean value and doesn't mutate the file, and WriteToFile is a command. It changes the file and its return type is void. So, these two methods follow the CQS principle. However, there's a problem with this code. The result of the query can become stale by the time the client code invokes the command. There could be some other process intervening down code between these two calls, and it can delete the file after the query is called, but before we invoke the command, and so to avoid this problem, we have to violate the command-query separation principle and come up with a new version of the method, like this one. As you can see, instead of checking for the file existence, it tries to update it, and if there's no such file, it gets an exception, catches it, and returns a failed result. The operation is atomic now. That's how we avoid information staleness. The downside here is that this method no longer follows the CQS principle. Other examples where the command-query separation principle is not applicable involve multi-threaded environments where you also need to ensure that the operation is atomic. However, it's still a good idea to make the CQS principle your default choice, and depart from it only in exceptional cases, like those I described above.

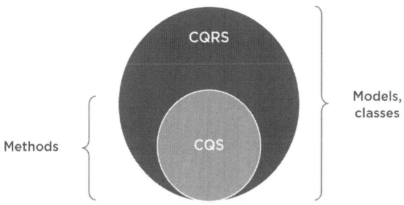

Methods

Models, classes

So what's the relation between CQS and CQRS? CQRS takes this same idea and extends it to a higher level. Instead of methods like in CQS, CQRS focuses on the model and classes in that model, and then applies the same principles to them.

- CQS
  - Method-command
  - Method-query
- CQRS
  - Command model
  - Query model

Just like CQS encourages you to split a method into two, a command and a query, CQRS encourages you to untangle a single, unified domain model and create two models: one for handling commands or writes, and the other one for handling queries, reads. Like I said, the principle is extremely simple. However, it entails very interesting consequences. So let's discuss them next.

Why CQRS?

- Performance
- Scalability
- Simplicity

Alright, so CQRS is about splitting a single model into two; one for reads and the other one for writes, but of course, this is not the end goal in and of itself. So what is it then? What are the benefits the CQRS pattern provides?

- Scalability : Create, Read, Update, Delete

First of all, it's scalability. If you look at a typical enterprise level application, you may notice that among all operations with this application, among all those create, read, update, and delete operations, the one that is used the most is usually read. There are disproportionately more reads than writes in a typical system, and so it's important to be able to scale them independently from each other.

- (Create, Update, Delete) :   Command side : 1 server
- (Read)   :   Query side : 10 servers

For example, you can host the command side on a single server, but create a cluster of 10 servers for the queries. Because the processing of commands and queries is fundamentally asymmetrical, scaling these services asymmetrically makes a lot of sense, too.

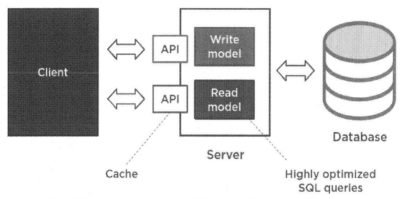

Cache   Server   Highly optimized SQL queries

Secondly, it's performance. This one is related to scalability, but it's not the same thing. Even if you decide to host reads and writes on the same server, you can still apply optimization techniques that wouldn't be possible with a single unified model. For example, just having a separate set of APIs for queries allows you to set up a cache for that specific part of the application. It also allows you to use database-specific features and hand-crafted, highly sophisticated SQL for reading data from the database without looking back at the command side of the application where you probably use some kind of ORM, but probably the most significant benefit here is simplicity. The command side and the query side have drastically different needs, and trying to come up with a unified model for these needs is like trying to fit a square peg in a round hole. The result always turns out to be a convoluted and over-complicated model that handles neither of these two parts well.

- Commands : Changing data
- Queries : Reading data
- Offloading complexity
- SRP applied at the architectural level

And often, the very act of admitting that there are two different use cases involved allows you to look at your application in a new light. By making the difference between them explicit and introducing two models instead of just one, you can offload a lot of complexity from your code base. Now all of the sudden, you don't need to worry about handling two completely different use cases with the same code. You can focus on each of them independently and introduce a separate solution that makes the most sense in each particular case. You can view this as the single responsibility principle applied at the architectural level. In the end, you get two models, each of which does only one thing, and does it well. So, to summarize, we can say that CQRS is about optimizing decisions for different situations. You can choose different levels of consistency, different database normal forms, and even different databases themselves for the command and query sides, all because you are able to think of commands and queries and approach them independently. You will see all these benefits in action when we'll be working on the sample project.

CQRS in the Real World

You might not realize it, but you probably have already employed the CQRS pattern in one form or the other in the past. Let's look at some examples from real-world projects.
- ORM for writing
- Raw SQL with JDBC for reading

If you ever used Entity Framework or Hibernate for writing data to the database, and raw SQL with plain Java JDBC for reading it back, that was CQRS right there. You probably thought at the moment that the necessity to drop the ORM and resort to the bare SQL for reads is just that, the necessary evil, a trade-off you have to make in order to comply with the performance requirements, but, no. This is a perfectly legitimate pattern, CQRS that is. Also, if you ever created database views optimized for specific read use cases, that was a form of CQRS as well. Another common example is ElasticSearch or any other full-text search engine. It works by indexing data, usually from a relational database, and providing rich capabilities to query it. That's exactly what CQRS is about. You have one model for writes and a completely separate model for reads, except that in this particular case, you don't build that second model yourself, but leverage an already-existing software.

Summary

- **Command Query Responsibility Segregation (CQRS) originates from the Command Query Separation Principle (CQS)**
  - **CQRS extends CQS to the architectural level**
  - **Split a unified domain model into two: for commands and for queries**
- **CQRS allows us to make different decisions for reads and writes**
  - **Better scalability**
  - **Better performance**
  - **Simpler code**

- CQRS is SRP applied at the architectural level
- Examples of CQRS in the real world

In this module, you learned that Command Query Responsibility Segregation is a pattern originating from the command-query separation principle. CQRS extends CQS to the architectural level. Just like CQS encourages you to split a method into two methods, a query and a command, CQRS encourages you to untangle a single, unified domain model and create two models: one for handling commands, and the other one for handling queries. CQRS allows us to make different decisions for reads and writes, which in turn brings three benefits: scalability, performance, and the biggest one, simplicity. You can view CQRS as the single responsibility principle applied at the architectural level. In the end, you get two models, each of which does only one thing, and does it really well. We also discussed examples of applying the CQRS pattern in the real world. ElasticSearch and database views are among them. In the next module, we will look at a sample project that's implemented without the CQRS pattern in mind. We will analyze it, discuss its drawbacks, and then start making steps towards implementing CQRS.

Module 2 : Introducing a Sample Project

Introduction

In this module, we will take a look at the sample project. I will guide you through its code base, and we will talk about its purpose and the underlying problem domain.

Problem Domain Introduction

The application we'll be working on is the API for a student management system. Here's the domain model of this system.

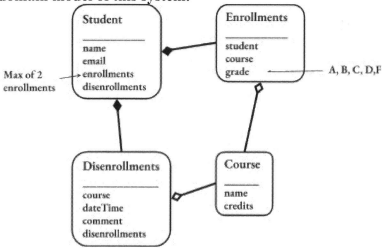

This is the main class in our model, Student. It consists of a name, email, collection of enrollments, and a collection of disenrollment comments. We'll get back to this one in a moment. A student can have up to two enrollments in courses. Each enrollment has a grade: either A, B, C, D, or F. The courses themselves have a name and the number of credits students receive for them. Whenever the user deletes an enrollment, he or she must specify the reason why the student wants to discontinue taking this course. This is what the disenrollment class is for. It shows which course was discontinued, the date and time of when this happened, and the comment from the student. All fields are mandatory. It means that when you create an enrollment, you must specify the student's grade, and when you delete one, you have to type in the comment from the student. The database pretty much mimics this domain model. I'll show it to you shortly. The API exposes the standard CRUD operations: the standard create, read, update, and delete. Here you can see a user interface that works with our API.

| Enrolled in: | | ⌄ | Number of courses: | ⌄ | Search |

| Create Student | Update Student | Delete Student |

Name	Email	First Course	Second Course	
Alice	alice@gmail.com	Calculus	Chemistry	
		Grade: A	Grade: C	
		Credits: 3	Credits: 3	

Note that this UI is for visualization purposes only. It's easier to follow the changes in an API project when you see how they affect the user experience. We will not be dealing with the code of the UI in this course, only with the API underneath it. Also note that, it could desktop application or a web one, written in JavaScript. It works with the API by parsing and sending JSON messages, just like a regular web application would. Alright, so you can see here a list of students with a single student, Alice. The list shows the students' names, emails, and the courses they are enrolled in. Students can be enrolled in only two courses, and so they are displayed here right away, in separate columns. Those columns contain the name of the course, the grade the student received, and the number of credits this enrollment provided. Note that the grade is taken from the enrollment database table, whereas the number of credits comes from the course table. So this is the read operation. The application provides the create, update, and delete operations, too. Let me show them to you.

Name:	Bob
Email:	bob@outlook.com
First course:	Literature
First course grade:	A
Second course:	Trigonometry
Second course grade:	B

| OK | Cancel |

When we create a student, we need to specify a name and an email. Let it be Bob and bob@outlook. com, and we can also indicate the student's enrollments. Although these fields are optional, we could leave them empty. So, let's say that Bob has chosen Literature

and received an A for it, and let's also say that he's chosen Trigonometry as his second course, and had a B for it.

Enrolled in:		Number of courses:		Search

Create Student	Update Student	Delete Student

Name	Email	First Course	Second Course
Alice	alice@gmail.com	Calculus Grade: A Credits: 3	Chemistry Grade: C Credits: 3
Bob	bob@outlook.com	Literature Grade: A Credits: 4	Trigonometry Grade: B Credits: 4

Saving this, and you can see the new student has appeared in the list. Now as the student exists, we can update it.

Name:	Bob

Email:	bob@outlook.com

First course:	Calculus

First course grade:	C

Second course:	Trigonometry

Second course grade:	B

OK	Cancel

Name	Email	First Course	Second Course	
Alice	alice@gmail.com	Calculus Grade: A Credits: 3	Chemistry Grade: C Credits: 3	
Bob	bob@outlook.com	Calculus Grade: C Credits: 3	Trigonometry Grade: B Credits: 4	

For example, we can change the enrollment from Literature to Calculus, the grade, and if I reopen it, you can see that the change is persisted successfully.

Name: Bob

Email: bob@outlook.com

First course:

Disenrollment comment: Don't want to take this class anymore

Second course: Trigonometry

Second course grade: B

OK   Cancel

We can also delete the enrollment. To do that, we need to select the empty option from the list of courses. When we do that, the application tells us to provide a disenrollment comment, and this comment is mandatory. If I try to save the form without it, the API

returns an error, and the UI displays it in this message box. Don't want to take this class anymore, and click OK.

Name	Email	First Course	Second Course
Alice	alice@gmail.com	Calculus Grade: A Credits: 3	Chemistry Grade: C Credits: 3
Bob	bob@outlook.com	Trigonometry Grade: B Credits: 4	

And you can see that Bob now has only one course. Calculus has been removed from his list of enrollments. Note that although we deleted the first course, the UI shows the empty slot in the second one. That's because, from our system's perspective, there is no difference in the order in which the student enrolls in the courses. And so the course that was the second one becomes the first, after we remove the enrollment. The field for the course grade shows up automatically when I try to create a new enrollment, and it's mandatory, too. If I try to save the form without it, the API also returns an error. Alright, along with all these features, the API exposes some pretty sophisticated search functionality in here. We can ask it to return only students who are enrolled in a specific course, and we can also request students who are enrolled in a particular number of courses. For example, I can choose Calculus, and the application shows that only Alice is enrolled in it. If I select Microeconomics, no

one is in here, and if I ask for students who
are enrolled in exactly one course, you can see
that the UI shows us Bob, and if I select two,
it's Alice, just as we would expect. Finally, we
can delete a student. Here I can select Bob,
and click Delete. Alright, let's now look at the
code.

Application Code Introduction

We have two projects: one for API and Logic,
and another for UI(static web project). Here's
the content of the API project, and the Logic
one. Let's look at the domain model first. This
is the course class.

```
package logic.students;
@Entity
public class Course {
    @Id
    @GeneratedValue
    private long id;
    private String name;
    private int credits;
    public String getName() {
        return name;
    }
    public void setName(String name) {
        this.name = name;
    }
    public int getCredits() {
        return credits;
    }
    public void setCredits(int credits) {
        this.credits = credits;
    }
}
```

Pretty straightforward, as you can see; just the name and the number of credits. Its mapping is straightforward, too.

I'm using Spring Boot JPA with Hibernate as the ORM and Hibernate mapping. Spring Boot will automatically create tables using annotations. And here's our main domain class, Student.

```java
package logic.students;
import java.util.ArrayList;
import java.util.List;
@Entity
public class Student {
    @Id
    @GeneratedValue
        private long id;
    private String name;
    private String email;
    private List<Enrollment> enrollments =
new ArrayList<Enrollment>();
    private List<Disenrollment>
disenrollments = new
ArrayList<Disenrollment>();
    protected Student() {}
    public Student(String name, String email)
{
        this.name = name;
        this.email = email;
    }
    private Enrollment getEnrollment(int
index) {
        if (enrollments.size() > index)
            return enrollments.get(index);
        return null;
    }
    public void
removeEnrollment(Enrollment enrollment){
        enrollments.remove(enrollment);
    }
```

```
        public void
addDisenrollmentComment(Enrollment
enrollment, String comment){
        Disenrollment disenrollment = new
Disenrollment(enrollment.getStudent(),
enrollment.getCourse(), comment);
        disenrollments.add(disenrollment);
    }
    public void enroll(Course course, Grade
grade) throws Exception{
        if (enrollments.size() >= 2)
            throw new Exception("Cannot have
more than 2 enrollments");
        Enrollment enrollment = new
Enrollment(this, course, grade);
        enrollments.add(enrollment);
    }
}
```

It consists of name and email. It also has a
collection of enrollments.

```
package logic.students;
@Entity
public class Enrollment{
        @Id
    @GeneratedValue
        private long id;
    private Student student;
    private Course course;
    private Grade grade;
    protected Enrollment() {}
    public Enrollment(Student student,
Course course, Grade grade) {
        this.student = student;
        this.course = course;
        this.grade = grade;
    }
    public void update(Course course, Grade
grade) {
        this.course = course;
```

```java
            this.grade = grade;
        }
        //getters and setters
    }
    enum Grade {
        A(1), B(2), C(3), D(4), E(5), F(6);
        private int value;
        public int getValue() {
            return value;
        }
        private Grade(int value) {
            this.value = value;
        }
    }
```

Each enrollment represents a link between a student and a course, with some grade. The grade is an enum that can be either A, B, C, D, or F. Aside from constructors, there's also an Update method that updates the course the student is enrolled in and the grade. By the way, the pattern you see here is a good way to work with collections in domain classes. The List field is what the ORM maps to when loading enrollments from the database, but instead of exposing this collection as is, you make it private and create a wrapper property around it with the type List, which shows the client code that it cannot modify this collection and have to use separate methods for that. Because there can be only two enrollments per student, there are two helper properties in here: first enrollment, and second enrollment. They use this getEnrollment method in order to return the appropriate enrollment. If there is no enrollment with such an index, the method returns null. Note that despite this invariant for having maximum of two enrollments per student, the product owner stated that this limit could be increased at some point in the future. Hence this collection of enrollments, and not just two properties here and in the database. We don't want to put ourselves in a difficult position by denormalizing the database prematurely, because it would be hard to add more enrollments in this case. Alright, there's also a collection of disenrollments here. These are, as you remember, for the comments the student provides when they disenroll from the course.

```java
package logic.students;
import java.util.Date;
@Entity
public class Disenrollment {
        @Id
     @GeneratedValue
     private long id;
     private Student student ;
     private Course course ;
     private Date dateTime ;
     private String comment ;
  Disenrollment(){}
  public Disenrollment(Student student,
Course course, String comment){
     this.student = student;
     this.course = course;
     this.comment = comment;
     this.dateTime = new Date();
  }
  //getters & setters
}
```

Here is its content: the student, the course, the date and time, and the comment itself. Back to the Student. Here, you can see two constructors: one for the ORM, which is non-public, and the other one for the client code, which shows that in order to create a student, it needs to provide a name and an email. Note that in a real-world application, you would want to validate these two strings and probably even wrap them into value objects. I'm omitting this for brevity. Along with the above properties, we also have three public methods. removeEnrollment deletes an enrollment from the student, addDisenrollmentComment is for adding a comment when the student disenrolls, and enroll is for creating an enrollment. Note check here. If the number of enrollments is already two or more, we throw an exception. This way, we ensure that the domain model maintains its invariants and always resides in a valid state. Here is the mapping for the student entity. Id, two properties, and two collections. Resharper tells me that this is unnecessary. Okay, this part of the mapping tells Hibernate to map directly to the backing field. The inverse setting, that this side of the relationship is not the one that determines the value of the studentID column in the Student database table, and Cascade. AllDeleteOrphan that Hibernate needs to delete all enrollments and disenrollments from the database when we delete them from these collections. Okay, let's now review the API project.

```
package api.controllers;
@RestController
@RequestMapping("api/students")
public class StudentController {
    private UnitOfWork unitOfWork;
    private StudentRepository
studentRepository;
    private CourseRepository
courseRepository;
    public StudentController(UnitOfWork
unitOfWork) {
        unitOfWork = unitOfWork;
```

```
        studentRepository = new
StudentRepository(unitOfWork);
        courseRepository = new
CourseRepository(unitOfWork);
    }
    @GetMapping()
    public List<StudentDto> GetList(String
enrolled, int number){
    return
convertToDtos(studentRepository.getList(enr
olled, number));
  }
    private List<StudentDto>
convertToDtos(List<Student> students){
    //convert student to studentDto
  }
    @PostMapping()
    public void create(@RequestBody
StudentDto dto) {
        Student student = new
Student(dto.Name, dto.Email);
        if (dto.Course1 != null &&
dto.getCourse1Grade() != null) {
            Course course =
courseRepository.getByName(dto.getCourse1(
));
            student.enroll(course,
dto.getCourse1Grade());
        }
        if (dto.Course2 != null &&
dto.getCourse2Grade() != null) {
            Course course =
courseRepository.getByName(dto.getCourse2(
));
            student.Enroll(course,
dto.getCourse2Grade());
        }
        studentRepository.save(student);
        unitOfWork.commit();
```

```java
    }
    @DeleteMapping("{id}")
    public void delete(long id){
    Student student =
studentRepository.getById(id);
        if (student == null)
            return Error($"No student found for
Id {id}");
        studentRepository.delete(student);
        unitOfWork.commit();
    }
    @PutMapping("{id}")
    public void update(long id,
@RequestBody StudentDto dto){
        Student student =
studentRepository.getById(id);
        if (student == null)
            return Error($"No student found for
Id {id}");
        student.setName(dto.getName());
        student.setEmail(dto.getEmail());
        Enrollment firstEnrollment =
student.getFirstEnrollment();
        Enrollment secondEnrollment =
student.getSecondEnrollment();
        if
(hasEnrollmentChanged(dto.getCourse1(),
dto.getCourse1Grade(), firstEnrollment)){
            if (dto.getCourse1().isEmpty()) { //
Student disenrolls
            if
(dto.getCourse1DisenrollmentComment().isE
mpty())
                return Error("Disenrollment
comment is required");
            Enrollment enrollment =
firstEnrollment;

student.removeEnrollment(enrollment);
```

```
        student.addDisenrollmentComment(enrollme
nt, dto.getCourse1DisenrollmentComment());
        }
        if (dto.getCourse1Grade.isEmpty())
            return Error("Grade is required");
        Course course =
courseRepository.getByName(dto.Course1);
        if (firstEnrollment == null){
            // Student enrolls
            student.enroll(course,
dto.getCourse1Grade());
        }else{
            // Student transfers
            firstEnrollment.update(course,
dto.getCourse1Grade());
        }
    }
    if
(hasEnrollmentChanged(dto.getCourse2(),
dto.getCourse2Grade(), secondEnrollment)){
        if (dto.Course2().isEmpty()) { // Student
disenrolls
            if
(dto.getCourse2DisenrollmentComment().isE
mpty())
                return Error("Disenrollment
comment is required");
            Enrollment enrollment =
secondEnrollment;

student.removeEnrollment(enrollment);

student.addDisenrollmentComment(enrollme
nt, dto.getCourse2DisenrollmentComment());
        }
        if (dto.getCourse2Grade().isEmpty())
            return Error("Grade is required");
```

```
        Course course =
courseRepository.getByName(dto.getCourse2(
));
        if (secondEnrollment == null){
            // Student enrolls
            student.enroll(course,
dto.Course2Grade());
        }else{
            // Student transfers
            secondEnrollment.update(course,
dto.Course2Grade());
        }
    }
    unitOfWork.Commit();
}
    private boolean
hasEnrollmentChanged(String
newCourseName, String newGrade,
Enrollment enrollment) {
        if (newCourseName.isEmpty() &&
enrollment == null)
            return false;
        if (newCourseName.isEmpty() ||
enrollment == null)
            return true;
        return newCourseName !=
enrollment.getCourse().getName() ||
newGrade !=
enrollment.getGrade().toString();
    }
}
```

And here is the StudentController, which contains the actual application functionality. It accepts a unit of work, which is a wrapper on top of Hibernate's session and transaction, and creates two repositories. The getList method is what returns the students to display in the data grid on the UI. It accepts two filter parameters: the name of the course the

student is enrolled in, and the total number of
courses.

```java
package logic.students;
public class StudentRepository {
    private UnitOfWork unitOfWork;
    public StudentRepository(UnitOfWork
unitOfWork) {
        unitOfWork = unitOfWork;
    }

    public List<Student> getList(String
enrolledIn, int numberOfCourses){
    Queryable<Student> query =
unitOfWork.query<Student>();
    if (!enrolledIn.isEmpty()){
        query = query.Where(x =>
x.enrollments.any(e =>
e.getCourse().getName() == enrolledIn));
    }
    List<Student> result = query.toList();
    if (numberOfCourses != null){
        result = result.Where(x =>
x.getEnrollments().size() ==
numberOfCourses).toList();
    }
    return result;
  }

    public Student getById(long id) {
        return
unitOfWork.get<Student>(id);
    }
    public void save(Student student) {
        unitOfWork.saveOrUpdate(student);
    }
    public void delete(Student student) {
        unitOfWork.delete(student);
    }
}
```

```
class CourseRepository {
    private UnitOfWork unitOfWork;
    public CourseRepository(UnitOfWork
unitOfWork) {
        unitOfWork = unitOfWork;
    }
    public Course getByName(String name) {
        return
unitOfWork.query<Course>().singleOrDefaul
t(x => x.getName() == name);
    }
}
```

Here's the repository method that does the
actual filtration. We first form an Queryable
that represents a SQL query Hibernate will
generate for the database. If the course name
is specified, we build up this query by adding
a Where clause to it. After that, we force
Hibernate to execute it and give us the
resulting list of students, and then if the
second filter is set, we return only students
who have this exact number of courses.
Alright, so after the repository returns us all
those domain objects, we convert them into
DTOs, data transfer objects, and return to the
client. The DTO looks like this.

```
package api.dtos;
public class StudentDto {
    private long id;
    private String name;
    private String email;
    private String course1;
    private String course1Grade;
    private String
course1DisenrollmentComment;
    private int course1Credits;
    private String course2;
    private String course2Grade;
```

```
    private String
course2DisenrollmentComment;
    private int course2Credits;
    //getters & setters
}
```

It contains and id, name, email of the student, and it also contains the information about his two courses. The Create method creates a student. It accepts this same DTO back. It reads the name and the email from it and uses them to instantiate a student. If the first course name and its grade is set up, the API finds this course, and enrolls the student to it. Note that here we are parsing the incoming grade, which is string, into the enum, and we do the same for the second course enrollment. After that, we save the student, commit the transaction, and return OK to the client. The delete method is pretty straightforward, too. It finds the student by the id and deletes it. The main complexity lies in the update method. Here, we also find the student, update their name and email, and then start the synchronization process. We first determine whether there are differences between the incoming DTO and the existing first enrollment. For that, we are using this private method, hasEnrollmentChanged. If the incoming enrollment course name is empty and the existing enrollment is empty, too, we consider this as no change. If one of them is empty and the second one is not, or if the course name or grade differ, it means the user has updated the enrollment. So, after we ensured that there is indeed a change to this enrollment, we need to decide which one is that. If the incoming course name is empty, that means the student disenrolls, and we need to check that the disenrollment comment is provided. If so, we remove the enrollment from the student, and add a disenrollment comment. Next, if the incoming course is not empty, it means one of two things: either the student enrolls in a new course or updates an existing enrollment. In either case, we need to make sure that the grade is provided. After that, we get the course from the database by its name, and check to see if the existing enrollment is null. If it is, it means that the student enrolls. If not, that they update the existing enrollment, and let me actually inline this variable. There is no need to have a separate one here. And we do the same procedure for the second enrollment. Let me inline the variable here, too. Okay. After the synchronization is done, we commit the transaction, and return success to the caller. Alright, that's it for the application functionality. Let's glance over the rest of the code real quick. You saw the student DTO already. It contains all the fields required to display a student in the grid, and update it when posting the changes back to the server. SessionFactory is a class that we use to generate Hibernate sessions. There should be only one such class in the application, hence we add it as a singleton. UnitOfWork is a wrapper on top of sessions themselves and should be instantiated and disposed of on each web request. The Student table consists of the id, name, and email. Enrollment references the student and the course, and it also has a grade which is represented as integer. Disenrollment, all the same fields as in the domain model, and the course. Alright, that's it for the application code base. Let's now talk about its drawbacks.

Application Code Drawbacks

I'm sure you have worked with such CRUD-based applications a lot in the past, so much that you might not even realize that there is something wrong with this code base. So, what is it? As we discussed in the first module, CQRS brings us three benefits: scalability, performance, and simplicity. Scalability is something we will talk about later in this course, and it's not obvious that this application suffers from scalability issues anyway, so let's skip it for now. What about performance? Well, let's open the StudentRepository once again.

```
public List<Student> getList(String
enrolledIn, int numberOfCourses){
        Queryable<Student> query =
unitOfWork.query<Student>();
        if
(!StringUtil.isNullOrWhiteSpace(enrolledIn)){
        query = query.where(x =>
x.getEnrollments().any(e =>
e.getCourse().getName() == enrolledIn));
        }
        List<Student> result = query.toList();
        if (numberOfCourses != null){
        result = result.where(x =>
x.getEnrollments().size() ==
numberOfCourses).toList();
        }
        return result;
        }
```

This is the method that filters the existing students by courses that they are enrolled in and the total number of such courses. What can you tell about its performance? Up to this moment, this method operates upon an Queryable, which is good because all the statements made upon an Queryable object translate into the corresponding SQL. It means that this Where statement, this filtration, is done in the database itself, which is exactly what we want.

 List<Student> result = query.toList();

But here, we force the ORM to fetch all the students with this course into memory, and only after that, continue narrowing them down. It means that the database will send us an excessive amount of data, which we then filter manually in the memory. This is a suboptimal solution and can hit the performance quite badly. It's not noticeable in our sample application, of course, but that's because there are just a few students in our database. In a real-world project, with hundreds of thousands or even millions of records, it would. Ideally, you should transfer only the minimum amount of data between the server and its database. But why are we doing that? Why force the ORM to fetch all data from the database on this step?

result = result.where(x => x.getEnrollments().size() == numberOfCourses).toList();

It's because we wouldn't be able to do this filtration otherwise. Neither Hibernate nor Entity Framework support filtering by the number of elements in a one-to-many relationship (Student 1 <=> N Enrollments), and so the only possible solution here is to finish up this filtration in the memory, using the in-memory provider. Another performance problem which comes up quite often is the problem called N+1 (N+1 query problem). It's when the ORM first fetches the students, and then for each of them performs a separate call to retrieve their enrollments, and then another one to get each of the corresponding courses. So instead of just one database roundtrip, you end up with several of them, and the more students there are, the more roundtrips you will have. In most cases, you can overcome this problem by instructing the ORM to include the navigation properties into the SQL script and fetch them along with the main object, but it's not always possible, and it's very easy to overlook this issue when relying on the ORM to query the database. Alright, and what about the code complexity? Is our code well-structured and easy to understand? Not really. Look at the Update method of StudentController once again. The fact that it is so long and that there are deep indentations is a sign that something is not right, and indeed, we are trying to do too many things here. Look at the section starting from this if statement. If there is no first course in the incoming student DTO, we disenroll the student from it. Otherwise, we either try to enroll the student in, or modify the enrollment, and the same for the second course. We could probably simplify this code by removing the duplication between the first and the second courses, but still, even with only a single such if statement, there is just too much going on here. This method clearly violates the single responsibility principle, one of the SOLID principles from Bob Martin. Another hint that tells us about the violation is this StudentDto. It is a jack-of-all-trades. It's used for both sending the data to the client, and receiving it back when updating the student. And because of that, some of the fields here remain unused in certain scenarios.

For example, when updating the student, the user needs to only specify either a grade or a disenrollment comment, but not both. And there is no need to fill out the credits fields because we don't update them on the server. They are used for displaying information on the UI only. This is a very CRUD approach, and it's not the best way to organize the application code. What we are doing here is we essentially merge all the possible modification to the students into a single giant update method, whereas each of those modifications should have their own representation. This artificial merge of responsibilities entails increase of complexity, which in turn, damages the code base maintainability. This is especially painful in long-running projects where complexity tends to pile up over time and at some point becomes so immense that the whole application moves to the category of legacy applications. It's still valuable for the business, but no one dares to touch it as every modification is likely to introduce new defects.

- **Domain-Driven Design and CQRS helps tackle complexity**

It's important not to allow such a growth of complexity, and Domain-Driven Design in general, and CQRS in particular, are very good at it. We will start untangling our code base in the next module. This thinking in terms of create, read, update, and delete operations is called CRUD-based thinking, and it often goes together with the anemic domain model. Anemic domain model is when you have domain classes that contain data and services classes that contain operations upon this data, but this is not always the case, and it's certainly not the case in our situation.

- Our this current Application is CRUD-based thinking but It is not Anemic domain model

In fact, our domain model is organized quite well and mostly encapsulated. If you look at the student entity, you can see that both collections are hidden from the client code so that it's impossible to modify them. The collections the clients of this class see are both read-only and don't have a setter. The parameter-less constructor is hidden. We expose a nice rich constructor instead that accepts both name and email, which explicitly tells the client code that these two pieces of data are required in order to create a new student. And we also have public methods that check for invariant violations. For example, before enrolling the student in a new course, this method validates the number of existing enrollments. We do have public setters in the name and email properties, but that's only because I have skipped the validation of this data for brevity. And because there's no validation needed, it's okay to keep these setters public. In a real-world application, you would probably want to wrap these properties into value objects. The only issue with regards to encapsulation is in these two methods(removeEnrollment and addDisenrollmentComment of Student class). Because they are always used together, you always need to add a disenrollment comment when you remove an enrollment. It would make sense to merge these two methods into a single one, but this issue is easy to fix. Other than that, the encapsulation here is pretty solid. Our domain model is not anemic.

Summary

- Introduced the sample application
- Drawbacks:

    - Single model for both reads and writes
    - CRUD-based thinking

- Inability to optimize the database queries

    - ORM doesn't support the required kind of querying
    - N+1 problem

- Unnecessary increase of complexity

    - All student modifications reside in a giant update operation
    - Violation of SRP

In this module, you saw the initial version of the application we'll be working on throughout this course. The two major drawbacks with it are the use of the single model for both reads and writes, and the CRUD-based thinking. The first issue leads to inability to optimize the database queries. You saw that we had to fetch an excessive amount of data from the database because the ORM doesn't support the kind of querying we need. It's also easy to fall into the N+1 problem where you end up with multiple roundtrips to the database instead of just one. The second issue leads to unnecessary increase of complexity. Because the application tries to fit all operations into the narrow box of create, read, update, and delete operations, what we end up with is the merging of all student modifications into a single giant update method. Another way to look at this problem is view it as the violation of the single responsibility principle; CRP for short. The Update method does too many things at once, which is never a good thing. In the next module, we will start the refactoring away from CRUD-based interface towards task-based interface. You will see how it simplifies the code base and helps improve the user experience.

Module 3 : Refactoring Towards a Task-based Interface

Introduction

In this module, you will learn the difference between the task-based interface and the CRUD-based one. You will also see how we transform the latter into the former.

CRUD-based Interface

One of the most widely spread problems in enterprise-level development is the way programmers approach data modification. As we discussed in the previous module, all operations in an application, fundamentally fall into one of the four categories: create, read, update, and delete; CRUD for short. And it's true. Technically, everything we do is either create, read, update, or delete something, but nevertheless, it's never a good idea to organize your application along these lines, except for the simplest cases. In fact, such an organization can have a devastating effect on your system, and not only in terms of its maintainability. It damages the user experience, too, as you will see in a second. We will call this approach to code design CRUD-based interface, and the overarching mentality, CRUD-based thinking. So, what's the problem with it, exactly? There are three of them. The first one is uncontrolled growth of complexity.

- Growth of complexity

    - Too many features in a single method
    - Increase in number of bugs

As you saw in the previous module, capturing in a single method all operations that somehow mutate an object, leads to enormous expansion of that method. At some point the complexity becomes unbearable. This, in turn, entails lots of bugs when modifying something in the code base and failures to meet project deadlines and quality standards. And this point comes much sooner than you might realize. Even our quite simple application exhibits those traits. Imagine how it would look if we add a few more pieces of data with their own business rules to the student class. The second problem is the disconnect between how the domain experts view the system and how it is implemented.

- Experts' view != Implementation

    - Experts don't speak in CRUD terms
    - Lack of ubiquitous language

Your domain experts don't speak in CRUD terms, and if they do, it's because you trained them to, not because it's natural for them. Think about it. When you go to college for the first time, does the administrator tell you that she will go ahead and create you in their system? No. She will tell you she is going to register you, not create, and if you decide to take a Calculus course, does she describe it as updating you? Absolutely not! What nonsense. She will enroll you in this course, not update. Another way to describe this problem is as lack of ubiquitous language. Ubiquitous language is one of the three pillars of Domain-Driven Design. It's essential for any enterprise-level development to set up a proper communication channel between the programmers and domain experts, and the best way to do so is to impose a single, unified ubiquitous language within a bounded context, and then have both domain experts and programmers speak this language. And not only speak, but use in it code, too, when defining the APIs of the system. And by the way, if you wonder what the remaining two pillars are, they are bounded contexts and the focus on the core domain.

- Lack of unified language leads to Maintainability issues

    - Have to translate from experts' language
    - Reduces capacity to understand the task

Just as the growth of complexity, this disconnect also leads to maintainability issues. Because there is no consistency between your code and the language of domain experts, you have to translate what those experts tell you every time you speak to them, and this mental overhead is a huge problem. It reduces your capacity to understand the task at hand and leads to inaccuracies in the implementation. On the other hand, elimination of this barrier can make wonders, and so you should always strive to remove as many of such inconsistencies as possible. The third problem is damaging the user experience.

- Damaging the user experience

    - The user has to investigate the interface on their own

You see, the problem of the CRUD-based thinking never stays within the boundaries of your application code. It also affects the UI. The CRUD-based thinking spills over from the code to the user interface, and the same issues that plague the code itself infect the user experience, too. Look at our application for example. If I try to update the student, does it really make sense that when I change the course enrollment to any other course, the interface stays the same, but as soon as I select the empty value, the grade goes away, and I suddenly have to provide the disenrollment comment? Not at all. What's happening here is because there are too many features lumped together on a single screen, the user has to figure them all out on their own. The user is like Sherlock Holmes here. He has to investigate the interface and deduce all the pieces of functionality on a large and complicated scene. Look at this screen once again. How many features are in here? At least four.

- Editing personal information
- Enrolling into a new course
- Transferring to another course
- Disenrolling from a course

Editing the student's personal information, enrolling them into a new course, transferring to another course, and disenrolling them from a course, and it will take a while for a user to uncover them all. Because of that, users have a hard time building a proper mental model of the product and grasping even the most common procedures. In complicated systems, many users never master all of those procedures, even after working with the software for a long time. All these features have to be separated out. The UI should guide the user through the process, not crash them with the full application functionality on a single giant window. Overall, the focus on user experience should become an integral part of the development process, which almost never happens when the CRUD-based thinking is in place.

- CRUD-based thinking affects

  - Code base
  - User experience

- CRUD-based interface affects

  - API
  - UI

As you can see, CRUD-based thinking affects both the code base and the user experience. This is why I call the end result CRUD-based interface; not user interface, but just interface. It's because this thinking affects both the API, application programming interface, and the UI, user interface. The two influence each other. If you have this problem with one, you will almost certainly have the same problem with the other. It's also interesting to take a short look at where this thinking originates from. Indeed, why is CRUD-based interface so widely spread? It's because of the programmers' desire to unify everything.

- OOP : Everything is an object

- CRUD-based thinking : Everything is CRUD

Just look at the premise of object-oriented programming, which states that everything is an object, and so why not take the same approach and define every operation in terms of CRUD, too? From the perspective of us as programmers, this leads to a nice-looking and clean system, where all of the APIs have one narrowly defined purpose. Who wouldn't like it? But of course, this doesn't lead anywhere. What you need to do instead is talk to domain experts, discover proper terms, and adjust your thinking accordingly.

Task-based Interface

So, how to fix this issue? The opposite of CRUD-based interface is task-based interface, and that's what we need to replace our current design with.

- Object = Task 1 + Task 2 + Task 3

  - Separate window
  - Separate API

Task-based interface is the result of identifying each task the user can accomplish with an object in the application. This is why it's name is task-based, and assigning a separate window to each of them, and by extension, introducing a separate API endpoint, too.

- Intuitive UI : Each window does one thing

  - Restore the single responsibility principle
  - Code base simplification
  - Improves user experience

This idea takes root in the concept of intuitive UI. Each window should implement a single distinctive operation. We need to restore the single responsibility principle, so to speak, and untangle our over-complicated update window and the giant update method. Not only will this lead to the code base simplification, but it will also bring a great amount of domain insight, just by virtue of implementing this separation, because you will have to research what each feature on the screen does and means to the domain experts. Because of all of that, you will be able to deepen your knowledge of the problem domain and bring your code base closer to the ubiquitous language. And the users will benefit greatly, too. The task-based interface makes it much easier for them to explore the software and learn what he or she can do with it. Currently, the application's business process is in the minds of people who developed it. Users must discover the correct process on their own. After moving towards the single responsibility principle and the task-based interface, each window on the screen becomes self-describing and intuitive.

Untangling the Update Method

- **Object-centric :**

Name:	Alice
Email:	alice@gmail.com
First course:	Calculus
First course grade:	A
Second course:	Chemistry
Second course grade:	B

OK	Cancel

- **Task-centric :**

  - **Editing personal info**
  - **Enrolling into a course**
  - **Transferring**
  - **Disenrolling from a course**

Alright, here's our update window again.
Currently, it is object-centric, meaning that it
tries to deal with the whole student object.
What we need to do instead is split it into
several task-centric windows, each
accomplishing its own separate task. As we
discussed before, there are four of such tasks.

Editing the student's personal information, enrolling into a new course, transferring to another course, and disenrolling from a course. So, let's do that. Here's our Update method of StudentController class. Note that these comments here are trying to translate for the reader what is going on in this method. For example, if there's no incoming course name, it means that the student disenrolls. If no enrollment currently exists, that means the student enrolls, and so on. This is already a sign that the method does too many things. We will untangle the method by extracting all these pieces of functionality into their own API endpoints. We'll start off with the enrollment. I'm naming the new method, Enroll.

```
@PostMapping("{id}/enrollments")
public void enroll(@PathParam("id") long id,
@RequestBody StudentEnrollmentDto dto){
Student student =
studentRepository.getById(id);
    if (student == null)
        return Error("No student found with
Id '{id}'");
    Course course =
courseRepository.getByName(dto.getCourse()
);
    if (course == null)
        return Error("Course is incorrect:
'{dto.getCourse()}'");
    boolean success =
Enum.tryParse(dto.getGrade());
    if (!success)
        return Error("Grade is incorrect:
'{dto.getGrade()}'");

    student.enroll(course, grade);
    unitOfWork.commit();
```

```
}
public class StudentEnrollmentDto {
private String course;
private String grade;
//getters & setters
}
```

Just like the update one, it will accept the student id and some DTO. This DTO, however, should be different. It should contain only the information about the enrollment, nothing more. So, I'm renaming this copy to StudentEnrollmentDto. Getting rid of this, the class will consist of a course name and a grade. We don't need anything else for the enrollment process, so I'm removing the remaining properties. Alright, the first step would be to fetch the student from the database and return an error if such student doesn't exist. Here is the old code once again. In order to enroll the student, we need to retrieve the course from the database and parse the grade. So let's do that. Get the course by its name. If such course doesn't exist, return an error saying that the course is incorrect. Next, parse the grade. If unsuccessful, also return an error and tell the client that the grade they passed in is invalid. Finally, student.enroll. Good, and commit the transaction and return a success. Very good. We can remove this part from update method of StudentController . The next method is going to be student transfer. So let's create another API endpoint, I'm calling the second endpoint Transfer.

```
@PutMapping("{id}/enrollments/{enrollment
Number}")
public void transfer(@PathParam("id") long
id, @PathParam("enrollmentNumber") int
```

```
enrollmentNumber, @RequestBody
StudentTransferDto dto){
 Student student =
studentRepository.getById(id);
    if (student == null)
        return Error("No student found with
Id '{id}'");
    Course course =
courseRepository.getByName(dto.getCourse()
);
    if (course == null)
        return Error("Course is incorrect:
'{dto.getCourse()}'");
    boolean success =
Enum.tryParse(dto.getGrade());
    if (!success)
        return Error("Grade is incorrect:
'{dto.getGrade()}'");
    Enrollment enrollment =
student.getEnrollment(enrollmentNumber);
    if (enrollment == null)
        return Error("No enrollment found
with number '{enrollmentNumber}'");
    enrollment.update(course, grade);
    unitOfWork.commit();
}
public class StudentTransferDto {
private String course;
private String grade;
//getters & setters
}
```

It will accept the student id as the first
parameter, but aside from that, we also need
to specify an enrollment number. This number
would tell us which of the enrollments the
student wants to modify. We didn't need this
number before because the Update method
accepted information about all enrollments in
a single DTO class, but because we are

untangling that class, the UI will have to indicate which of the enrollments is changing. Alright, and of course, we will also need a DTO. I'm copying the StudentEnrollmentDto, because it has the same properties we need, and renaming it to StudentTransferDto. Note that these two classes are exactly the same, and so in theory, we could use the same DTO for both endpoints. However, this is generally a bad practice, because it introduces coupling between the two endpoints. Now if the parameters required for one operation change for some reason, and we modify this DTO, the second API endpoint will automatically change its input parameters, too. That is something you want to avoid.

- Don't-repeat-yourself principle = Domain knowledge duplication

Also, there is no violation of the don't-repeat-yourself principle here. These two classes just happen to coincide with regards to their structure. There is no domain knowledge duplication. So, the Transfer method will accept this new DTO. We will need the same validations as in the Enroll method so I am copying them here. Now, we need to get the enrollment itself from the student somehow, and currently, we only have these first and second enrollment properties. We need to adjust the student class a little bit. As you can see, the code is already there. The two helper properties use the method that accepts the enrollment number. So we just need to make this method public. Now we can use this method in the controller. Passing the number, and introducing a variable. If the number is incorrect, we are returning an error. After all the preparations are done,Fixing the parameter, and the enrollment, and also committing the transaction . We can remove this piece of code from update method,. The next one is student disenrollment, So I'm calling the third method Disenroll.

```
@PostMapping("{id}/enrollments/{enrollment
Number}/deletion")
public void disEnroll(@PathParam("id") long
id, @PathParam("enrollmentNumber") int
enrollmentNumber, @RequestBody
StudentDisEnrollmentDto dto){
 Student student =
studentRepository.getById(id);
     if (student == null)
         return Error("No student found with
Id '{id}'");
     if
(StringUtil.isNullOrWhiteSpace(dto.getComm
ent()))
         return Error("Disenrollment comment
is required");
     Enrollment enrollment =
student.getEnrollment(enrollmentNumber);
     if (enrollment == null)
         return Error("No enrollment found
with number '{enrollmentNumber}'");
         student.removeEnrollment(enrollment);

student.addDisEnrollmentComment(enrollme
nt, dto.getComment());
     unitOfWork.commit();
}
public class StudentDisEnrollmentDto {
private String comment;
//getters & setters
}
```

Here is the binding for it. It will also accept the student id and the enrollment number. As

56

for the DTO, it will be StudentDisenrollmentDto, and it will have a single parameter, this comment from here, using it here. Alright. The first validation is also about the student. Aside from that, we need to ensure that the comment is not null or empty. Getting the enrollment by the enrollment number, and the action. Removing the enrollment, and adding a disenrollment comment. Changing the property. Note that here, we are using two methods from the domain model to accomplish a single task.

```
student.removeEnrollment(enrollment);
student.addDisEnrollmentComment(enrollment, dto.getComment());
```

This is a code smell. It is a sign that the domain model is not properly encapsulated and is leaking internal implementation details. And indeed, neither of the two operations make sense without the other one from our domain model's perspective. We cannot remove an enrollment without adding a disenrollment comment, and we cannot add a disenrollment comment without removing an enrollment.

Student.java :

```
public void removeEnrollment(Enrollment enrollment, String comment){
        enrollments.remove(enrollment);
        Disenrollment disenrollment = new Disenrollment(enrollment.getStudent(), enrollment.getCourse(), comment);
        disenrollments.add(disenrollment);
}
```

StudentController.java : disEnroll method :

```
 student.removeEnrollment(enrollment, dto.getComment());
```

So let's fix this. I'm moving the code from the add disenrollment comment method and removing addDisenrollmentComment method altogether. Fixing the parameters, and removing the invocation, student.addDisEnrollmentComment(enrollment, dto.getComment()); . Very good. Now it's impossible to do one action without the other. Remove these lines in update method of StudentConroller. We extracted all of its functionality of update method into separate API methods Alright, the last piece of functionality is editing the student's personal information. Introducing a new method for it.

```
@PutMapping("{id}")
public void editPersonalInfo(@PathParam("id") long id, @RequestBody StudentPersonalInfoDto dto){
 Student student = studentRepository.getById(id);
     if (student == null)
         return Error("No student found with Id '{id}'");
     student.setName(dto.getName());
     student.setEmail(dto.getEmail());
     unitOfWork.commit();
}
public class StudentPersonalInfoDto {
private String name;
private String email;
//getters & setters
}
```

The binding is going be the same as for the update one. As for the DTO, we only need a name and an email. So I'm adding a new DTO containing these two properties. Copying this code from update method , and committing the transaction. Now we can get rid of the whole update API endpoint. We have extracted all the functionality out of it, and this private method

(hasEnrollmentChanged).So remove this
hasEnrollmentChanged method too.

Recap: Untangling the Update Method

- Untangled the student update method

  - Editing personal information
  - Enrolling into a new course
  - Transferring to another course
  - Disenrolling from a course

- Simplified the code base

In the previous demo, you saw how we untangled the student update method. We have split it into four methods, each implementing its own distinctive task. Editing the student's personal information, enrolling into a new course, transferring to another course, and disenrolling from a course. In other words, we refactored the update API endpoint, which had a CRUD-based interface into several smaller ones, which are now task-based. Each of those methods adheres to the single responsibility principle, meaning that they are responsible for doing one task and one task only. That, in turn, allowed us to greatly simplify those methods. Look at the disenroll one for example, and now compare it to only a part of the update method. The cyclomatic complexity of this one, which you can measure by counting the number of indentations in code, is higher here, and it's longer, too. It's much harder to understand what is going on here, whereas the new method is simple and straightforward. The cyclomatic complexity here is low. The singular indentations are related to input validation, and you can see a clear pattern in all of the four methods. First, we do the validation, which takes some space, but is simple to follow nevertheless. Then, we delegate the actual work to the domain model, and after all that, commit the transaction and return the response to the client. Note that along with the API endpoint, we modified the DTOs we are using, too. Before the refactoring, the Update method relied on this large and clunky StudentDto in which we lumped together fields to accommodate all possible modifications that could be done to the student. And not only that, we used this same DTO for displaying students' info in the grid. Hence even more fields that are unnecessary when updating the student. The new task-based interface now has a separate DTO for each of the tasks. All of them are small and concise and have only the info required to accomplish the task at hand. We have removed all the redundancies from the DTO, and instead of one coarse-grained, one-size-fits-all class, have several fine-grained ones.

- Avoid DTOs that are full of "holes".

The takeaway here is this. Avoid DTOs that are full of holes, and holes here mean fields that are not used in 100% cases. They are a strong sign you have a CRUD-based interface. This simplicity is an inherent part of the task-based interface. Because we don't try to fit all modifications into a single giant update method anymore, we are able to come up with a much more precise and straightforward solution. Each task provides us with the right level of granularity and intent when modifying data. Alright, so we were able to simplify our code after refactoring towards the task-based API. Let's now see how this change affects the user interface.

Task-based User Interface

I won't bother you showing how I'm refactoring the UI. After all, this course is not about user interfaces, but it's still interesting to look at the end result, so here it is.

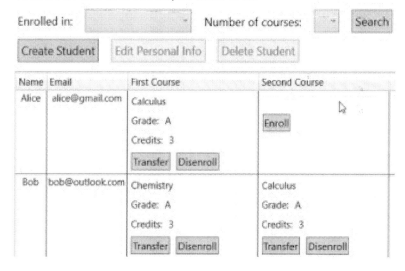

First of all, you can see that I have renamed this button to Edit Personal Info. It was Update Student previously.

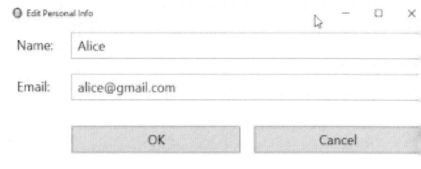

And if I click it, it shows me a much simpler window with just the personal information of the student. The rest of the functionality is now represented as context-dependent buttons in the grid itself. For example, Alice is not enrolled in her second course, and so here you can see this button, which I can use to enroll Alice in a new course.

And this window is very small, too. All fields here are dedicated to accomplishing this specific task, enrolling the student in some course, which makes the interface simple and intuitive. Let me refresh the grid. The two remaining actions show up only when they are applicable in the current context; that is, when the student is already enrolled in some course. You can see that I can transfer Alice from Literature to, say, Microeconomics, or I can disenroll her from this course, in which case I need to specify a disenrollment comment.

Note that this comment is the only piece of information I need to provide when disenrolling the student, which makes a lot of sense if you think about it. Everything else can be deduced from the context. No need to explicitly specify the course she is disenrolling from. So, when I type in some comment, and refresh the grid, you can see the second course is gone now, and the application offers me to enroll Alice again. This natural flow of events makes for a great user experience. Every single operation is intuitive and asks for the minimum amount of information to accomplish the task at hand. Now compare it to the old version with the CRUD-based UI. All four operations are lumped together on a single big screen. The controls appear and disappear depending on the user input, and it's not obvious at all that if I select an empty string for the first course, it means that I'm disenrolling the student.

Dealing with Create and Delete Methods

Alright, we've dealt with the Update method. We extracted it into four smaller, task-based ones, but what about create and delete API endpoints of StudentController? At first glance, they seem fine. The Delete method is small and on point. It might look like the create method does too many things. After all, it both creates a student and enrolls them into courses, but actually, no. Having these two operations together helps user experience. Users normally perform these two actions, one after the other, and so having them on a single screen simplifies this task. There still are two problems with these methods, though. First, the Create endpoint still uses StudentDto to accept data from the outside. It is the same DTO the UI uses to display the students in the grid, and it has fields we don't need when creating a student, for example, id and course credits. So, we need to come up with a separate DTO that would contain only the fields required for this task.

- Create student ----->> Register student
- Delete student ----->> Unregister student

The second problem is the names of these methods themselves. Think about it. Does it make sense, from the domain's perspective, to create or delete a student? How do the domain experts describe these operations? Remember, any API endpoint that is named after one of the CRUD operations is a red flag, and each time you see such an endpoint, ask yourself, is this operation really just that, create or delete, or maybe there is a deeper meaning behind it? This habit alone can give you a great amount of insight into the problem domain you are working on. So, what do these methods actually mean? The only way to find out is to ask the domain experts. As we discussed earlier, they probably say something like register when they create a student, and unregister when they delete one. And so it makes sense to incorporate this piece of ubiquitous language into our code as well. Alright, let's do that.

```
public class NewStudentDto {
public String name;
public String email;
public String course1;
public String course1Grade;
public String course2;
public String course2Grade;
//getters & setters
}
@PostMapping()
public void register(@RequestBody
NewStudentDto dto) {
Student student = new Student(dto.getName(),
dto.getEmail());
if (dto.getCourse1() != null &&
dto.getCourse1Grade() != null) {
 Course course =
courseRepository.getByName(dto.getCourse1(
));
 student.Enroll(course, Enum.parse < Grade >
(dto.getCourse1Grade()));
}
if (dto.getCourse2() != null &&
dto.getCourse2Grade() != null) {
 Course course =
courseRepository.getByName(dto.getCourse2(
));
 student.enroll(course, Enum.parse < Grade >
(dto.getCourse2Grade()));
}
studentRepository.save(student);
unitOfWork.commit();
}
@DeleteMapping("{id}")
```

```
    public void unregister(long id) {
Student student =
studentRepository.getById(id);
if (student == null)
 return Error("No student found for Id {id}");
studentRepository.delete(student);
unitOfWork.commit();
}
```

Copying the DTO. Renaming it to NewStudentDto, and removing all fields we don't need. Id, disenrollment comments and course credits. Now we can use this DTO here. Renaming the Create method to register, and the Delete one to unregister. Very good. Note that we now use the StudentDto class only for displaying students in the data grid, and so, we can get rid of the fields that were used for modifying the students.

```
public class StudentDto {
public long id;
public String name;
public String email;
public String course1;
public String course1Grade;
public int course1Credits;
public String course2;
public String course2Grade;
public int course2Credits;
//getters & setters
}
```

In particular, we don't need the disenrollment comments anymore. And here's how the UI looks now. I modified it off-screen.

Name:	I
Email:	
First course:	
First course grade:	
Second course:	
Second course grade:	

OK   Cancel

The Register Student screen still contains all those fields, but no disenrollment comments anymore. Perfect. Our interface, both API and UI, is now completely task-based.

- Task-based Interface   != CQRS

  - Can have one with or without the other
  - CQRS often goes hand in hand with CQRS

Note, however, that task-based interface is not a prerequisite for CQRS per se. You can have one with or without the other, but the problem of CRUD-based thinking often goes hand in hand with CQRS. People who suffer from having a single model that handles both reads and writes usually also suffer from CRUD-based thinking. Also note that sometimes, CRUD-based interface is just fine. It's the same situation as with anemic domain models, really. If your application is not too complex, or you are not going to maintain or evolve it in the future, no need to invest in task-based interface. Basing your interface on CRUD operations can give a short-term boost, which might be helpful if the development of the application is not going to last long enough to justify the investment.

Summary

- Refactored towards task-based interface
- CRUD-based thinking: fitting all operations into CRUD terminology
- CRUD-based interface: result of CRUD-based thinking

    - "Interface" means both UI and API

- Problems with CRUD-based interface

    - Uncontrolled growth of complexity
    - Lack of ubiquitous language
    - Damaging the user experience

- Task-based interface

    - Result of identifying each task the user can accomplish with an object
    - Affects both UI and API

- Avoid CRUD-based language

  - A sign of CRUD-based thinking
  - Create & Delete -> Register & Unregister

- Avoid DTOs with "holes" in them

  - Example: DisenrollmentComment and Grade in StudentDto

In this module, you saw how we refactored our application towards task-based interface. You learned what CRUD-based interface and CRUD-based thinking is. CRUD-based thinking is when people try to fit all operations with an object into a narrow box of create, read, update, and delete operations. CRUD-based interface is the result of CRUD-based thinking. Note that the word interface includes both user interface, UI, and application programming interface, API. It's because the two influence each other. If you have this problem with one, you will almost certainly have the same problem with the other. There are three problems with CRUD-based interface. The first one is uncontrolled growth of complexity. You saw that capturing in a single method all operations that somehow mutate an object leads to this method being overcomplicated and hard to maintain. The second problem is the disconnect between how the domain experts view the system and how it is implemented. Your domain experts don't speak in CRUD terms. They don't say create or update a student, and just this act of listening to domain experts and trying to incorporate the business language into the application leads to great domain insights. The third problem is damaging the user experience. CRUD-based interface leads to too many features being lumped together on a single screen so that the user has to figure them all out on their own. The resulting UI is not intuitive. It is object-centric, meaning that it tries to deal with the whole object at once. Task-based interface is the opposite of CRUD-based interface. It is the result of identifying each task the user can accomplish with an object and assigning a separate window to each of them. This also affects both the UI and the API. In terms of the UI, the single object-centric window gets split into several task-centric ones. In terms of the API, you introduce several API endpoints dedicated to accomplishing one single task. As a result, both the UI and API becomes much simpler to understand and maintain. For example, you saw how we untangled the single update method into several much smaller ones and the UI started to make much more sense, too. Try to avoid CRUD-based language when it comes to naming your endpoints. It's a sign of CRUD-based thinking. For example, in our sample application, we renamed Create and Delete methods into Register and Unregister, because that's what they meant to the domain experts. Another sign of CRUD-based interface is when you have DTOs in which some of the fields are not used in 100% of cases. For example, the CRUD-based version of our application used the StudentDto class with the fields DisenrollmentComment and Grade. Those fields got populated in particular scenarios only and were left empty in all other cases. That's because our API was CRUD-based and tried to do too many things at once. In the next module, we will segregate commands from queries in our application, the essential part of the CQRS pattern.

Module 4 : Segregating Commands and Queries

Introduction

In the previous module, we refactored our application towards the task-based interface. All the operations the student can perform with it are now clearly defined and have their own API endpoints.

- Task-based interface ---->>> Explicit commands and queries

    - Scalability
    - Performance
    - Simplicity

Our next goal on the path to CQRS would be to introduce explicit commands and queries for each of those API endpoints. This will help us down the road by bringing in the benefits of CQRS; the three benefits we discussed in Module 1: scalability, performance, and simplicity.

Introducing a First Command

Alright, so in, our StudentController. Let's first outline which of the API endpoints here represent commands and which queries. As we discussed in the first module, any operation can be either a command or a query. A query doesn't mutate the external state, such as that of the database, but returns something to the caller. A command is the opposite of that. It does mutate the external state, but doesn't return anything to the client. So, which one is the getList method? The getList method is clearly a query. It returns a list of students that are enrolled in some course, if it's specified by the client, and that are enrolled in a particular number of courses. The method doesn't mutate any data. As you can see, all it does is it selects the students from the database and transforms them into DTOs, which are our data contracts. The Register endpoint, on the other hand, is a command. It does mutate the database state. It inserts a new student into it, and it doesn't return anything to the caller other than the acknowledgment of the operation success. So, I'm marking this method as a command. Unregister deletes the student from the database. So it's a command. The same is true for the Enroll method. Transfer is also a command. Disenroll and EditPersonalInformation. Both of those are commands, too. As you can see, the separation between the endpoints in terms of which falls to which category is pretty clear, and it aligns perfectly with the REST best practices. Put and Post http methods correspond to commands, while endpoints like GetList, which are marked with the GET http method, they are queries, and this alignment is not a coincidence. REST fundamentally follows the Command-Query Separation principle.

- **REST fundamentally follows the Command-Query Separation principle.**

If you execute a Get query, it should not modify the state of the REST resource, which is the same as executing a query in the CQS sense of that word, and if you run a POST, PUT, or DELETE query, that does change the state of the resource, and that would be a command in the CQS taxonomy. To continue down the CQRS path, we need to introduce separate classes for each command and query in our application, and so we will do exactly that. We'll start with the EditPersonalInfo method. Let's create a new class. I'm calling it EditPersonalInfoCommand.

```
package logic.students;
public class EditPersonalInfoCommand {
public long id;
public String name;
public String email;
//setters & getters
}
```

Make it public. Good. So the command will contain the data from the DTO, the name and email properties. And I also need to add the student id of type long.

StudentController.java :
```
public void editPersonalInfo(){
Command command = new
EditPersonalInfoCommand();
    command.execute();
}
```

Now, what we could do with this command is we could first instantiate it in the controller method, and then somehow execute, for example, by calling an Execute method on the command itself. That would be the first choice for most of us, programmers, who want to make sure that the command is properly encapsulated. However, this is not the best design decision, because we would conflate two different concerns here. Command itself should represent what needs to be done. It should be a declaration of intent, so to speak. The execution is a different matter. The execution often refers to the outside world, such as the database and third-party systems, and you don't want to delegate this responsibility directly to the commands. This is an important point, and we will talk about it in more detail later in this module. So, because we don't want the command to execute itself, there should be a separate class that does that, and here it is, EidtPersonalInfoCommand handler.

```
class EditPersonalInfoCommandHandler{
    public void
handle(EditPersonalInfoCommand
command){

    }
}
```

It will contain a single method, Handle, that accepts the command.

```
@PutMapping("{id}")
public void
editPersonalInfo(@PathParam("id") long id,
@RequestBody StudentPersonalInfoDto dto){
 EditPersonalInfoCommand command = new
EditPersonalInfoCommand();
 command.setEmail(dto.getEmail());
 command.setName(dto.getName());
```

```
command.setId(id);
EditPersonalInfoCommandHandler handler
= new EditPersonalInfoCommandHandler();
handler.handle(command);
}
```
What we can do now is we can instantiate that
handler in the controller, and pass the
command to it. Good. And of course, we need
to instantiate the command itself properly.
Setting the Email, Name, and Id, and let me
comment remaining code, and move it to the
handler itself. Now, the problem with this
design is that we need to instantiate the
handlers manually in each controller method,
which would be quite repetitive, or we would
have to inject them into the controller's
constructor. As you can see, there are quite a
few of controller methods here, and we would
need a handler for each of them, and so you
can imagine that the number of parameters in
the constructor will get out of control very
quickly. You don't want to find yourself in
this situation either, because that would
damage the maintainability of the code base.
What we can do instead is we can leverage the
dependency injection infrastructure, and we
will do that shortly. For now, get back to the
EditPersonalInfo method. Another problem
with this approach is that each handler class
will have their own public API. There would
be no common interface between them, and so
we won't be able to extend them with new
functionality. That's something we are going
to do moving forward, introduce decorators
on top of the command handlers so that we
could enrich those handlers and introduce
cross-cutting concerns to our application. And
so we need a common interface between all
our commands and command handlers. For

that, we need to introduce a couple new types. The first one is ICommand.

```
interface Command{}
```

It's a marker interface, which means that its sole purpose is to mark the commands in our code base, like this.

```
public class EditPersonalInfoCommand implements ICommand{
//
}
```

The second one is ICommandHandler.

```
interface ICommandHandler{
public void handle(ICommand command);
}
```

The interface will have just a single method, Handle, that would accept a command of type ICommand. Let me put the ICommandHandler interface closer to ICommand.

```
class EditPersonalInfoCommandHandler implements ICommandHandler{
private UnitOfWork unitOfWork;
public EditPersonalInfoCommandHandler(UnitOfWork unitOfWork){
 this.unitOfWork = unitOfWork;
}
    public void handle(EditPersonalInfoCommand command){
    Repository studentRepository = new StudentRepository(unitOfWork);
    Student student = studentRepository.getById(command.getId());
        if (student == null)
            return Error("No student found with Id '{id}'");
        student.setName(command.getName());
        student.setEmail(command.getEmail());
```

```
        unitOfWork.commit();
    }
}
```

Now we can inherit our command handler
from this interface and put the
EditPersonalInfo command as the type
parameter here. This way, all our command
handlers will have a common interface, which
would make it easy to decorate them later.
Alright, so having this groundwork laid out,
let's uncomment the code in the handler and
fix the compilation errors. As you can see
here, the handler needs a student repository.
In the controller, we create the repository in
the constructor, by instantiating it manually.
For that, we use an instance of UnitOfWork
that spring DI or any other dependency
injection injects into the constructor, and just
to remind you, UnitOfWork is our own
wrapper on top of Hibernate session and
transaction. So, we can apply the same
approach in the handler. I'm creating a
constructor that would accept a UnitOfWork,
and save it to the local field, making this field
ReadOnly. Good. Next, instantiating the
student repository in the handle method. Use
it here. Put command. Id instead of just id, the
same here, and get the name and the email
from command as well. Now, all the
compilation errors are fixed, except for
returning error. So, what are we going do
about it? If we look in the controller, and open
the definition of this method, you can see that
 It's basically a wrapper on top of the built-in
BadRequest action result, and we pass an
envelope with the error to it. We could make
our command handler return an instance of
IActionResult with bad request, too, but that's
not the best design decision. It's better to leave

the java concerns to the controller, and keep the command handler free of such concerns, but how can we return an error from the command handler then? That's a good question. One way could be to throw an exception, which is also not the best way to deal with this issue. Exceptions used for controlling the program flow and specifically for validation, tend to complicate the code base, and it's better to use an explicit return value instead. so we will use a special Result class. It's a simple class that represents either a success or a failure of an operation.

```java
interface ICommandHandler{
public Result handle(ICommand command);
}
class EditPersonalInfoCommandHandler
implements ICommandHandler{
private UnitOfWork unitOfWork;
public
EditPersonalInfoCommandHandler(UnitOfW
ork unitOfWork){
 this.unitOfWork = unitOfWork;
}
   public Result
handle(EditPersonalInfoCommand
command){
   Repository studentRepository = new
StudentRepository(unitOfWork);
   Student student =
studentRepository.getById(command.getId());
    if (student == null)
       return Result.fail("No student found
with Id '{id}'");
    student.setName(command.getName());
    student.setEmail(command.getEmail());
    unitOfWork.commit();
    return Result.oK();
 }
```

}
You can easily come up with an
implementation of your own. Now that the
Handle method returns a result instance, here,
we can call Result. Fail instead of error, and
we also need to update the signature of the
interface. Change the return type from void to
Result.
StudentController.java :

```
@PutMapping("{id}")
public IActionResult
editPersonalInfo(@PathParam("id") long id,
@RequestBody StudentPersonalInfoDto dto){
 EditPersonalInfoCommand command = new
EditPersonalInfoCommand();
 command.setEmail(dto.getEmail());
 command.setName(dto.getName());
 command.setId(id);
 EditPersonalInfoCommandHandler handler
= new
EditPersonalInfoCommandHandler(unitOfW
ork);
 Result result = handler.handle(command);
 return result.isSuccess ? ok() :
Error(result.error());
}
```

If we go back to the controller, we can
instantiate the handler, pass the UnitOfWork
instance to the constructor, get the result back
from the Handle method, and then parse it. If
the result is successful, call OK, and if not, call
Error with the error from the result instance.
Perfect, and of course, we also need to return
Result. Ok in the handler. That would mean
that everything worked fine.

Commands in CQS vs. Commands in CQRS

In the previous demo, we introduced our first command, EditPersonalInfo command, and a command handler for it.

- StudentController --->> EditPersonalInfoCommand + EditPersonalInfoCommandHandler

    - Moved all logic from controller to handler

We moved all the code from the corresponding controller method to that handler.

```
@PutMapping("{id}")
public IActionResult
editPersonalInfo(@PathParam("id") long id,
@RequestBody StudentPersonalInfoDto dto){
 EditPersonalInfoCommand command = new
EditPersonalInfoCommand();
 command.setEmail(dto.getEmail());
 command.setName(dto.getName());
 command.setId(id);
 EditPersonalInfoCommandHandler handler
= new
EditPersonalInfoCommandHandler(unitOfW
ork);
 Result result = handler.handle(command);
 return result.isSuccess ? ok() :
Error(result.error());
}
```

Now, all the method does is it instantiates the command and the handler for it, passes the former to the latter, gets a result out of the handler, and then interprets that result by returning either a 200 or a 400 response; 200 being a success, and 400 being a validation error here. Before we move forward, let's clarify some potentially confusing terminology. You might have noticed that we've been using the term Command in two different ways.

- Command

  - Controller method

    - @PutMapping("{id}") public IActionResult editPersonalInfo(@Path Param("id") long id, @RequestBody StudentPersonalInfoDto dto){/*...*/}
    - CQS command

  - Class

    - public class EditPersonalInfoComma nd implements ICommand{/*...*/}
    - CQRS command

First, the controller method, and second, the command class. The difference between them is that the former is a command in the CQS sense. Remember, we discussed in the first module that the command-query separation principle states that all methods in a class should be either commands or queries. This method is a command because it modifies the application's state and doesn't return any data to the client aside from the confirmation that the operation is completed successfully. The second one, the class, is a command in the CQRS sense. It's an explicit representation of what needs to be done in the application. It's a simple class named after the operation; in our case, the EditPersonalInformation operation, and it contains the data required to perform that operation: the id, the name, and the email of the student. You can think of commands as being serializable method calls. So, there should be no confusion, really. It's just the term Command is overloaded and has many meanings depending on the context you operate in, and the same is true for queries. The term query is also overloaded and means a query-method in the context of CQS, and a class in the context of CQRS. Alright, so a command is a serializable method call, so to speak.

```
class EditPersonalInfoCommandHandler
implements ICommandHandler{
    public Result
handle(EditPersonalInfoCommand
command){
    Repository studentRepository = new
StudentRepository(unitOfWork);
    Student student =
studentRepository.getById(command.getId());
        if (student == null)
            return Result.fail("No student found
with Id '{id}'");
        student.setName(command.getName());
        student.setEmail(command.getEmail());
        unitOfWork.commit();
```

```
    return Result.oK();
  }
}
```

Here you can see our command handler again.
The most fascinating part here is that that
single method(handle()) is also a command in
the CQS sense, because it mutates state and
doesn't return anything aside from the
operation confirmation. It's interesting to see
how these concepts are interconnected with
each other.

Commands and Queries in CQRS

Now that we have our first command, let's
discuss commands and queries in more detail.

- Messages

    - Commands : Tell the
      application to do something
    - Queries : Ask the application
      about something
    - Events : Inform external
      applications

All messages in an application can be divided
into three categories: commands, queries, and
events. A command is a message that tells our
application to do something, a query is a
message that asks our application about
something, and an event is an informational
message. Our application can generate an
event to inform external applications about
some change.

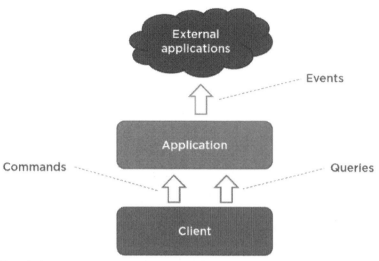

Here's how all three can be depicted together on a single diagram. As you can see, the client sends commands and queries to our application in order to either tell it to do something or ask about something. On the other end, our application communicates with external applications via events. It informs them about changes within the app. We will not be focusing on events much in this course. Just keep in mind that it's the same concept as domain events. You can learn more about domain events in my other book , Domain-Driven Design with Spring Boot. There are naming guidelines associated with all these three types of messages.

- Commands

    - Imperative tense
    - EditPersonalInfoCommand

- Queries

- Start with "Get"
- GetListQuery

- Events

  - Past tense
  - PersonalInfoChangedEvent

First of all, commands should always be in the imperative tense. That's because they are telling the application to do something. EditPersonalInfoCommand is a good example here. It tells our application to edit, to modify the personal information of the student. Queries usually start with the word Get, for example, GetListQuery. That's because queries ask the application to provide some data, and it's hard to come up with something else other than the word Get for such a request. Finally, events should always be in the past tense. That's because they state a fact that already happened; some event that is significant for your domain model. For example, let's say that our application needs to convey to the marketing department the updates to the students' email addresses, so that the marketing department has correct contact information to send promotional materials to. To do that, we could raise a domain event, something like PersonalInfoChangedEvent, and the marketing department could subscribe to that event and update their records accordingly.

- Command

- Edit personal info
- Server can reject a command

- Event

  - Personal info changed
  - Server can't reject an event

Note the difference in the semantics here, EditPersonalInfo versus PersonalInfoChanged. This distinction is very important. By naming the command Edit Personal Information, you imply that the server can reject this message. It can reject executing it, for example because the email in that command is invalid. On the other hand, the application cannot reject an event. If your application receives an event named PersonalInfoChanged, there is nothing it can do about it. The operation it informs you about has already happened, and this event is just a notification about that fact. The only thing the application can do is update its records, and so naming in either imperative or past tense makes it absolutely clear which message that is. It makes it clear whether the message is a command or an event.

- Commands should use the ubiquitous language
- CRUD based thinking

  - CreateStudentCommand
  - UpdateStudentCommand
  - DeleteStudentCommand

Another important guideline with regards to the command names is that they should use the ubiquitous language. If you see a command named CreateStudent or UpdateStudent, it's a sign of the CRUD-based thinking, and, as we discussed in the previous module, it leads to the CRUD-based interface, which is hard to maintain and work with. Make sure your commands are task-oriented, not CRUD-oriented. We already solved this problem in the last module. All our API endpoints are task-oriented, so I won't dwell on it too much here. And one last thing about naming.

- EditPersonalInfoCommand
- GetListQuery
- PersonalInfoChangedEvent
- Naming convention is enough to distinguish between them

You saw that I used postfixes when naming commands, queries, and events; the Command, Query, and Event postfixes. However, it's perfectly fine to leave them out. If you follow the above guidelines and always name the commands in the imperative tense, events in the past tense, and start queries with Get, you shouldn't have any problems with distinguishing these three types of messages, and so there's no need really in keeping the postfixes. It's your call, though. If you are more comfortable with keeping them, it's fine, too.

Commands and Queries in the Onion Architecture

You might remember this diagram from my Domain-Driven Design with Spring Boot.

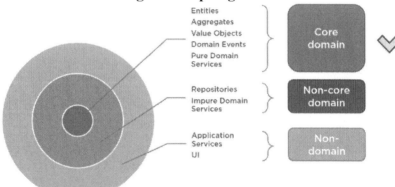

It's the onion architecture that shows elements of a typical application. The inner layer represents the core of the domain model. It's the entities, aggregates, value objects, domain events, and pure domain services with which you model the domain. This is the most important part of your system, the one that you need to pay attention to the most. One level beyond that, there are parts of the domain model that touch the external world; the database, third-party systems, the file system, and so on. Finally, there are other application services and the UI, which don't belong to the domain model. Such layering helps show the relationship between different parts of the application. The fact that the core domain resides in the center of the onion means that classes from it cannot access classes from the outer layers. The core domain should be isolated from the external world. It should be self-sufficient. Alright, so where do commands and queries belong in this picture? Think about it for a moment. Okay. You actually had a hint here. Events are already presented on this diagram, and they are located at the core layer of the onion, and that's right; commands and queries also belong to that layer, just like domain events.

- All messages are part of the core domain
  - Command = An operation to do
  - Query= A question to ask
  - Event= An outcome for external apps

All messages in your application are part of the core domain model. They explicitly represent what the clients can do with the application; that would be the commands. What questions they can ask that would be the queries, and what the outcome is for the external applications. That's the events. You might be hesitant to treat commands and queries as part of the core domain, and if you are, consider this.

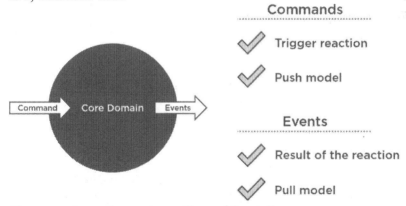

Commands and events really reside at the same abstraction level of the workflow. Commands are what trigger a reaction in the domain model, and events are the result of that reaction. They are the two ends of the same stick. The only difference between them is that the commands follow the push model, while the events, the pull one. In other words, it's someone else, not our application, that raises the commands. That would be the push model, and, on the other hand, it's us, our application, that raises the events. That is the so-called pull model.

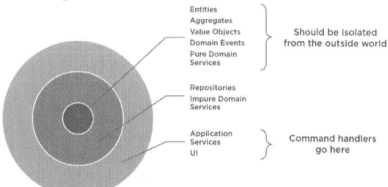

And when you start looking at commands and queries as parts of the core domain, it becomes clear why you shouldn't implement the handling logic in those commands and queries themselves. It's all about domain model isolation. The classes inside the core domain shouldn't refer to the outside world, because that would violate the domain model isolation. Those classes should only know about classes in the same layer. They should know nothing about the external world or the classes in the outer layers of the onion. At the same time, when you handle a command, you do need to refer to the external world, or to the outer layers of the onion. In our case for example, we edited the personal info of the student, and to do that, we worked with the student entity itself, and we also worked with the repository, and that repository talked to the database, a component that is external to the core domain. Alright, but where to attribute the handlers then, you might ask? That's a good question. They implement the same role as the Application Services do, so command handlers should go here, to the Application Services layer, and if you remember, before we introduced the EditPersonalInfo command handler, the code that was responsible for handling this scenario resided in the controller, and this controller is part of our Application Services layer. So when we moved this code to the handler, we just relocated it from one part of the Application Services layer to another.

Commands vs. DTOs

Let's now talk about the difference between commands and DTOs, data transfer objects. Look at our EditPersonalInfo controller method once again.

```
@PutMapping("{id}")
public IActionResult
editPersonalInfo(@PathParam("id") long id,
@RequestBody StudentPersonalInfoDto dto){
 EditPersonalInfoCommand command = new
EditPersonalInfoCommand();
 command.setEmail(dto.getEmail());
 command.setName(dto.getName());
 command.setId(id);
 IHandler handler = new
EditPersonalInfoCommandHandler(unitOfW
ork);
 Result result = handler.handle(command);
 return result.isSuccess ? ok() :
error(result.error());
```

}
Here, we are accepting a DTO from the client, and then transform it into a command. The reason why people don't often attribute commands to the core domain is that they often replace the DTO with the command itself. They skip this mapping stage, and transform the controller into something like this

```
@PutMapping("{id}")
public IActionResult editPersonalInfo(
@RequestBody EditPersonalInfoCommand
command) {
IHandler handler = new
EditPersonalInfoCommandHandler(unitOfW
ork);
Result result = handler.handle(command);
return result.isSuccess ? ok() :
error(result.error);
}
```

And so in this case, because the commands come from the outside of our application, it would indeed be problematic to treat them as part of the core domain model. The solution to this problem is that you shouldn't do that.

- Commands and DTOs tackle different problems

Commands and DTOs are different things. They tackle different problems.

- Commands

  - Serializable method calls

- DTOs

- Data contracts
- Backward compatibility

Remember, commands are serializable method calls, calls on the methods in the domain model, whereas DTOs are the data contracts. The main reason we introduce this separate layer with data contracts is to provide backward compatibility for the clients of our API.

- Commands <<------mapping-------->> DTOs

- Backward compatible
- Easy to refactor

Without the DTOs, our API will introduce breaking changes with every change of the domain model, or we will not be able to properly evolve the domain model because of the constraints imposed by the backward compatibility. Either way, using the commands in place of DTOs forces us to choose one of the two suboptimal design decisions. On the other hand, the DTOs and the mapping between them and the commands ensures that our application will be both backward compatible and easy to refactor.

- The use of commands as DTOs = The use of entities as DTOs

- Hinder refactoring

Using commands in place of DTOs is similar to using domain entities, which is extremely harmful for the encapsulation of your app. It's not as bad, of course, because commands themselves don't contain any business logic, but the drawbacks are very similar. Both of these approaches hinder your ability to refactor the domain model.

```
public class EditPersonalInfoCommand implemetns ICommand{
   private long id ;
   private String name;   //   FirstName LastName
   private String email;
   private EditPersonalInfoCommand(long id, string name, string email){
   this.d = id;
   this.name = name;
   this.email = email;
   }
}
```

- Can't modify the command

For example, if we decide to split the student name into first and last names, we won't be able to modify the command itself in order to keep the backward compatibility. We will have to keep the existing, obsolete version of the command, and implement the mapping in the handlers instead. It's much cleaner and more maintainable to just have two layers, the DTOs and the commands, each playing their own part. DTOs for backward compatibility where you can have as many versions of the data contracts as you want, and commands for the explicit representation of what the clients can do with the application. It's much easier to implement the mapping between the two than to try to lump all these responsibilities into the same class.

- DTOs = Backward compatibility
- Commands = Actions upon the application

Note that if you don't need backward compatibility in your application, then it's fine to use commands in place of DTOs.

- It's fine not to have DTOs if you don't need backward compatibility

    - A single client which you develop yourself
    - Can deploy both the API and the client simultaneously

For example, if you have a single client, which you also develop yourself, and you deploy both of them at the same time, then there is no such issue as breaking the clients of your API. Because both of them will have the latest version deployed simultaneously, there would be no such situation where you have an old version of the client talking to the new version of the API, but keep in mind that it's an edge case. Treat it as a code complexity optimization technique. In a case of publicly available API, or if you cannot deploy the client and the API simultaneously, you do need both, the DTOs and the commands.

Leveraging Spring to Resolve Command and Handlers pattern

I mentioned previously that it's not very convenient to create handlers in each and every controller action manually. We manually instantiate the handler, and then pass the command to it,. What we can do instead is we can leverage the Spring resolve the command handlers for us.

```java
@CommandHandler
public class EditPersonalInfoCommandHandl
er
 implements ICommandHandler<EditPersona
lInfoCommand, Result> {
@Autowire
UnitOfWork unitOfWork;
@Override
public Result
handle(final CreateNwUserCommand
command)       throws Exception {
Repository studentRepo = new
StudentRepository(unitOfWork);
    Student student = studentRepo
.getById(command.getId());
      if (student == null)
        return Result.fail("No student found
with Id '{id}'");
      student.setName(command.getName());
      student.setEmail(command.getEmail());
      unitOfWork.commit();
      return Result.oK();
}
}
```

To send a command, you need to send the object through the gate. To do so, inject the Gate dependency with @Autowired

```
@RestController
public class StudentController{
    @Autowired
    private Gate gate;
    @PutMapping("{id}")
    public IActionResult editPersonalInfo(
@RequestBody
 EditPersonalInfoCommand command) {
    Result result = gate.dispatch(command);
    return result.isSuccess ? ok() :
error(result.error);
    }
}
```

You have two possibilities to send a command :

- a synchronous way :
  gate.dispatch(command);
- an asynchronous way :
  gate.dispatchAsync(command);

The methods are returning the results of the command execution.

Introducing a Query

As you can see, it's quite useful to leverage the built-in Spring dependency injection container and Command and Handler pattern. It does exactly what we need with very little effort on our part. Let's now introduce a query. In our application, there is currently only one method that is a query in the CQS sense, and that is getList.
StudentController :
@GetMapping()

```
public IActionResult getList(String enrolled,
int number){
    List<StudentDto> dtos = convertToDtos(
studentRepo.getList(enrolled, number));
return ok(dtos );
}
```

As you can see here, it returns a list of student DTOs. So, let's go to our command. We will change this controller method.

```
public interface IQuery{}
public interface IQueryHandler{
    IResult handle(IQuery);
}
```

Here it is. Just like the ICommand interface, we need to create an IQuery one, and another interface for query handlers, where parameter should implement the IQuery interface. It will also have a single method handle. Instead of ICommand, the type of the input parameter will be IQuery Note that the command handler returns just a result instance, and that's fine, because commands generally don't return anything other than the confirmation of the operation success, or failure for that matter, but the query handler will have to provide some data, and that data will vary depending on the particular query. The query is going to be GetListQuery.

```
public class GetListQuery implement IQuery{
}
```

It will implement the IQuery interface of type list of student DTOs. Our command handler doesn't know about the StudentDto. That's because this DTO is defined in the API project. Ideally, all DTOs, all data contracts, should reside in their own assembly, and that would fix this error. Both API and Logic projects would then reference this separate project with data contracts. As you can see in the controller, the getList method has two parameters.

```
public class GetListQuery implement IQuery{
private String enrolledIn;
private int numberOfCourses;
//getters, setters and constructor for these two fields
}
@QueryHandler
public class GetListQueryHandler implement
IQueryHandler<GetListQuery,
List<StudentDto>>{
@Autowired
private UnitOfWork unitOfWork;
public List<StudentDto> handle
(GetListQuery query){
   Repository studentRepo = new
 StudentRepository(unitOfWork):
   List<StudentDto> dtos = convertToDtos(
studentRepo.getList(enrolled, number));
   return dtos;
   }
}

    @PutMapping("{id}")
    public IActionResult editPersonalInfo(
@RequestBody
 EditPersonalInfoCommand command) {
    Result result = gate.dispatch(command);
    return result.isSuccess ? ok() :
error(result.error);
    }
public class StudentController{
@Autowired
private Gate gate;
@GetMapping()
public IActionResult getList(String enrolled,
int number){
GetListQuery query = new
GetListQuery(enrolled, number);
```

```
Result result = gate.dispatch(query);
    return result.isSuccess ? ok() :
error(result.error);
    }
}
```

We will similarly refactor all other commands and query of this student management application.

Summary

- **Refactored towards explicit commands and queries**
- **Introduced unified interface for command and query handlers**
- **Leveraged Spring dependency injection and Command Query Handler Pattern mechanism for resolving the handlers**
- **Difference between commands and queries in CQS and CQRS taxonomies**

    - **CQS: command is a method that mutates state**
    - **CQRS: command represents what you can do with the application**

- **Command: serializable method call**
- **Command handler: an Spring controller with a single method that is a CQS command**
- **Messages: commands, queries, and events**

- Command tells the application to do something
- Query asks the application about something
- Event is an informational message

- Name all 3 types of messages properly:

  - Commands should be in the imperative tense
  - Events should be in the past tense
  - Queries: same as commands, start with "Get"

- Commands and queries in the onion architecture

  - Commands, queries, and events should reside in the core domain layer
  - Commands: push model
  - Events: pull model

- Commands vs DTOs

  - DTOs help achieve backward compatibility
  - Commands explicitly state what the application can do

In this module, we refactored our application towards using explicit commands and queries. All our application code now resides in separate command and query handler classes. We also introduced a unified interface for all our command and query handlers. This will help us in the next module when we'll be working on decorators for them. Spring core has a great dependency injection and Command Query Handler Pattern mechanism out of the box, and we've leveraged that mechanism for the handler resolution. Let's recap the key points of this module. First, the difference between commands and queries in CQS and CQRS taxonomies. In CQS, which stands for the Command-Query Separation principle, a command or a query is a method that either mutates the state of the application and doesn't return anything to the caller, or does return something, but doesn't leave any side effects in the application state. In CQRS, which stands for Command-Query Responsibility Segregation, a command or a query is a class that represents what you can do with the application. This class has a handler with a single Handle method, which also follows the CQS principle. It means that the Handle method of a CQRS command handler doesn't return anything to the caller, aside from the confirmation of the operation success or failure, and the Handler method of a Query handler doesn't incur any side effects. As you can see, the definitions are quite interconnected. You can view a CQRS command as a serializable method call and a command handler as a regular Spring controller with just a single method that is a command in the CQS sense. All messages in an application can be divided into three categories: commands, queries, and events. A command is a message that tells the application to do something, a query is a message that asks the application about something, and an event is an informational message. It tells external applications about some change significant to your domain. It's important to properly name all three types of messages. Commands should be in the imperative tense. They are telling the application to do something. This naming guideline also implies that your application can reject this message. On the other hand, an event is a message that should always be in the past tense. That's because it states a fact, something that already happened in the past. It also implies that there is nothing the application can do about this message. The change it informs about has already taken place. Queries should follow the same naming guideline as commands, except that in the vast majority of cases, they should start with Get. Always use the ubiquitous language when naming the messages. It will allow you to avoid the fallacy of the CRUD-based thinking that we discussed in the previous module. We discussed where to place commands and queries in the onion architecture. They should reside in the core domain layer, the same place the domain events belong in. The only difference between commands and events is that the commands follow the push model, whereas the events follow the pull one. It means that it's the other applications that trigger the commands, and it's your application that triggers the events. We talked about the differences between commands and DTOs. In a publicly exposed API, you need to have both. DTOs, data transfer objects, allow you to achieve backward compatibility, whereas commands allow you to explicitly state what your application can do. Don't combine these two responsibilities unless you don't need backward compatibility for some reason. In the next module, we will discuss how to implement decorators upon the command and query handlers. It can be a very powerful mechanism that allows you to achieve great flexibility with little effort and maintenance cost.

Module 5 : Implementing Decorators upon Command and Query Handlers

Introduction

In the previous module, we introduced explicit commands and queries in our code base and handlers for them.

- Commands and handlers   ------->> Enrichment of the handlers

In this module, I will show you how to enrich those handlers in a simple, yet very powerful way. You will see how the groundwork we have laid so far, allows us to easily introduce cross-cutting concerns in our application.

New Requirement: Database Retries

Let's say that we've got a new requirement. Our database goes offline from time to time, because the connection between the application and the database is unstable, and so we need to implement a retry mechanism to deal with this issue. Let's see we could do that. In the EditPersonalInfoCommandHandler. One way to implement this requirement in this particular handler would be to write something like this.
EditPersonalInfoCommandHandler.java :

```
public Result
handle(EditPersonalInfoCommand
command){
    Repository studentRepo = new
StudentRepository(unitOfWork);
    Student student =
studentRepo.getById(command.getId());
    if (student == null)
        return Result.fail("No student found
with Id '{id}'");
    student.setName(command.getName());
    student.setEmail(command.getEmail());
    for(int i=0;i<3;i++){
     try{unitOfWork.commit();}
     catch(Exception e){continue;}
    }
    return Result.oK();
}
```

Try to commit the transaction, say, three times. For that, we need to wrap the Commit method call into a try-catch statement. This commit method is where the database transaction gets committed and all the SQL

queries are executed. So if there is any connection interruption between the application and the database server, it will show up in this line. This approach sounds plausible at first, but unfortunately, it wouldn't work. First of all, when a database connection breaks up, the connection that our application keeps hold of becomes unusable. You cannot simply call the Commit method one more time. Even if the database goes online at that time, Java will throw an exception saying that this connection is broken, and that the recovery is not possible. So, you need to instantiate a new database connection on each attempt. Another issue here is that this Commit method is not the only one that reaches out to the database. We also have this line (Student student = studentRepo.getById(command.getId());) that retrieves the student. If for some reason, the student is no longer in the database between the first and the second attempt, you need to somehow show this fact and not just blindly keep retrying the operation. And so it turns out that the only reliable way to implement the retry is to re-run the command handler as a whole.
EditPersonalInfoCommandHandler.java :

```
public Result
handle(EditPersonalInfoCommand command)
{
 for (int i = 0; i < 3; i++) {
  try {
   Repository studentRepo = new
StudentRepository(unitOfWork);
   Student student =
studentRepo.getById(command.getId());
   if (student == null)
```

```
   return Result.fail("No student found with
Id '{id}'");
   student.setName(command.getName());
   student.setEmail(command.getEmail());
   unitOfWork.commit();
   return Result.oK();
  } catch (Exception e) {
   continue;
  }
 }
}
```

Re-run the full code of the handle method, which as you can see, is quite verbose, and in addition to that, it means a lot of code duplication. If we want to implement such a retry in any other command handler, we won't have any choice other than copying and pasting this loop with the try/catch statement in all of our handlers. Fortunately, there is a better way. As I mentioned in the previous module, we can take advantage of the unified interface all our command and query handlers implement, and introduce decorators on top of them. Let's implement such a decorator and after that, discuss what that is in more detail.

Introducing a Database Retry Decorator

Alright, so let's start with our first decorator. I'm creating a new folder for it, called Decorators, and a new class, DatabaseRetryDecorator, making it public .

```
package logic.decorators;
public class DatabaseRetryDecorator
implements ICommandHandler {
private ICommandHandler handler;
```

```
private Config config;
public
DatabaseRetryDecorator(ICommandHandler
handler, Config config) {
 config = config;
 handler = handler;
}
public Result handle(ICommand command){
    for (int i = 0; ; i++){
     try{
          Result result =
handler.handle(command);
          return result;
       }catch (Exception ex){
          if (i >=
config.getNumberOfDatabaseRetries() ||
!isDatabaseException(ex))
             throw new Exception();
       }
     }
   }
private boolean
isDatabaseException(Exception exception) {
 String message =
exception.getInnerException().getMessage();
 if (message == null)
   return false;
 return message.contains("The connection is
broken and recovery is not possible")
   || message.contains("error occurred while
establishing a connection");
}
}
```

It should implement the ICommandHandler
interface . The type argument itself should be
constrained to the ICommand interface.
Inside the handle method, we will introduce a
for loop that will retry the action for three
times(that we will read from configuration file

), and inside of it, there will be a try-catch statement, like this. This line is where we will do the retry itself. So, how to do the actual retry? We need a reference to the handler this decorator decorates, and how to get it? We can request it to be injected into the constructor. So, let's create one. Accepting another ICommandHandler saving this handler to a private field, and making this field ReadOnly. Now we can use this handler here, in the try-catch statement, handler. Handle, and return the result to the caller. So the idea here is to catch any exception that pops up from the handler and then, if it's related to the database connectivity issue, retry the same handle method once again, and we need to do that only if the number of attempts doesn't exceed three. Checking that the exception is indeed a database exception, if any of these conditions doesn't hold true, re-throw the exception. The check as to whether the exception is a database connectivity exception will look like this. It should always have an inner exception with one of these two strings. Another issue in this class is that we are using the magic number three here and here. It's better to extract it into a config file. . As we discussed previously, when the database becomes unreachable, you cannot reuse the existing connection, even if the database goes back online. And here you can see that the UnitOfWork class is just a wrapper on top of Hibernate's session. What we need to do instead is we need to inject the SessionFactory class in our handler and then instantiate the UnitOfWork manually. The session factory is a singleton. There is only one instance of it in our application, and we can use this instance to instantiate all our units of work. So let's replace the UnitOfWork with SessionFactory, save it to a local field, mark as ReadOnly, and we can now get rid of the UnitOfWork class in the constructor. What we can do instead is we can instantiate a new UnitOfWork in the handle method itself using the SessionFactory, and replace these two variables with it.

Decorator Pattern

In the previous demo, we implemented our first decorator, which detects database connectivity failures and re-runs the same command handler several times, until it either reaches the limit of three attempts or gets a successful result, meaning a result without an exception. Now that you saw the decorator pattern in action, it's time to discuss it in more detail.

- Decorator is a class or a method that modifies the behavior of an existing class or method without changing its public interface.

So, what is it? Decorator is a class or a method that modifies the behavior of an existing class or method without changing its public interface, and thus, without affecting the clients of that class or method. In our sample application, the decorator implemented the same ICommandHandler interface all other commands implement, but instead of being one of the true commands, so to speak, it enhanced their behavior with additional logic, and when doing so, it didn't require us to modify any of the clients of this command handler.No changes were needed in this class EditPersonalInfoCommandHandler , we get a decorator instance that wraps our handler and adds its own functionality on top of it.

- Decorators

  - Introduce cross-cutting concerns
  - Avoid code duplication
  - Adhering to the single responsibility principle

- Decorators

  - Technical issues

- Handlers

  - Business use cases

We can use Spring AOP to use decorators as in more declarative form.

Introducing Another Decorator

Let's say that we received another requirement, implement audit logging for our EditPersonalInfo command handler. The stakeholders want to have a track in our audit log of the changes people make to their personal information, and that's on top of the retry behavior we have at the moment.

Thanks to the mechanism we've developed, we know how to deal with this request, by adding a new decorator. So, let's do that. I'm adding a new class to our decorators folder called AuditLoggingDecorator.

```
package logic.decorators;
public class AuditLoggingDecorator
implements ICommandHandler {
private ICommandHandler handler;
public
AuditLoggingDecorator(ICommandHandler
handler) {
 handler = handler;
}
public Result Handle(ICommand command) {
 String commandJson =
JsonConvert.serializeObject(command);
 Console.witeLine("Command of type
{command.getType().getName()}:
{commandJson}");
 return handler.handle(command);
}
}
```

Just as our first decorator, it will implement the ICommandHandler interface. Implementing missing members, and injecting a handler in the constructor. Now, in the Handle method, we want to somehow log the incoming command to have the audit trail. One way to do so would be to serialize it into a JSON, and then log the resulting text, and of course, I'm using Console. WriteLine here just for brevity. In a real-world application, you need to inject a logger into the decorator the same way we did with the config instance in the previous decorator, and use that logger instead.

We can use Spring AOP to use decorators as in more declarative form.

Command and Query Handlers Best Practices

Alright, we are almost done with this module. The last thing I'd like to talk about is some of the best practices you could employ when implementing the CQRS pattern.

- How should you organize commands, queries, and handlers?

    - Orphaned commands and queries

The first one is how to organize commands, queries, and their respective handlers. It's often the case that as you develop your application and refactor it, you need to re-organize some of the commands and handlers, and maybe even remove some of them. Because commands and handlers are represented by different classes, and because they usually reside in different files, it's also often the case that when you delete a handler, you forget to delete the corresponding command or query, and so you can end up with some orphaned classes, some commands or queries without their handlers. Fortunately, it's quite easy to avoid this. You can nest the handler class inside the command class. So, take for example, our EditPersonalInfoCommand handler, and paste it here, and that's it. You can even make the handler non-public. I've put all of our commands into separate files, nested the handlers inside of them, and also grouped the commands into a separate folder. Now if you decide to remove a command handler, you will be able to immediately remove the commands, as well because it resides right there in the same class. This helps with discoverability and code cohesion, too. Also note that all the handlers are made internal, and so they don't even comprise the public API of this assembly.

- Don't reuse command handlers.

Alright, the second best practice I'd like to talk about is this. Don't reuse command handlers. It's sometimes tempting to do so when you have two similar use cases. In such a case, you might decide to create two command handlers, and call one of them from the other one, like on this diagram.

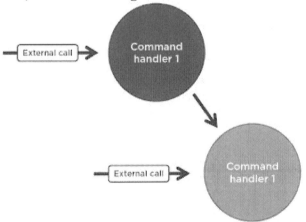

That is counterproductive, however. Here's an example. This is the UnregisterCommand handler.

```
class UnregisterCommandHandler
implements ICommandHandler{
        @Autowired
         private Gate gate;
        @Autowired
```

```
    private SessionFactory sessionFactory;
    public
UnregisterCommandHandler(SessionFactory
sessionFactory){
        sessionFactory = sessionFactory;
    }
    public Result
handle(UnregisterCommand command){
        UnitOfWork unitOfWork = new
UnitOfWork(sessionFactory);
        Repository repository = new
StudentRepository(unitOfWork);
        Student student =
repository.getById(command.Id);
        if (student == null)
            return Result.fail($"No student
found for Id {command.getId()}");
        gate.dispatch(new
DisenrollCommand(command.getId(), 0,
"Unregistering"));
        gate.dispatch(new
DisenrollCommand(command.getId(), 1,
"Unregistering"));
        repository.delete(student);
        unitOfWork.commit();
        return Result.ok();
    }
}
```

- **Misuse of commands**

It deletes a student from the database. You can see that I have added these two lines above in bold to disenroll the student from the existing courses before unregistering them. Let's just assume that business wants us to do that for some reason. This implementation looks quite reasonable at first, especially if you consider that we don't just call the

DisenrollCommand handler directly, but instead create proper commands and dispatch them via the dispatcher. The problem here is the misuse of commands.

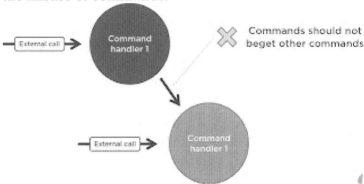

Commands should not beget other commands; that is contrary to the principle we discussed in the previous module. It's other applications that trigger commands, not our system. Our system reacts to those commands and produces domain events, and our system cannot create subsequent commands on its own. A command is a representation of what the clients can do with our application, and only clients can raise them.

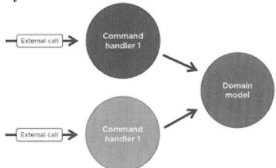

Alright, but how to reuse code then, you might ask? You have the domain model for that. Just extract the common code from the two handlers into a separate class, such as a domain service, and use it in both classes. This will have the same effect in terms of the code reuse, but without the downside of reusing the command handlers themselves.

Summary

- Used decorators to extend command and query handlers
- Decorator is a class that modifies the behavior of an another class without changing its public interface

    - Allows for introducing cross-cutting concerns without code duplication
    - Adherence to the single responsibility principle
    - Chaining multiple decorators together allows for introduction of complex functionality

- Best practices around working with command and query handlers

    - Put command and query handlers inside their respective commands and queries
    - Don't reuse command handlers

In this module, we discussed how to extend command and query handlers without code duplication and while keeping the handlers themselves simple. For that, we used decorators. Decorator is a class that modifies the behavior of an another class without changing its public interface. In other words, it's a wrapper that preserves the interface of the thing it wraps. It's a very powerful technique. It allows you to introduce cross-cutting concerns to your application without code duplication. It also allows you to adhere to the single responsibility principle, as you are able to separate the code of the cross-cutting concerns from the code that implements the actual business-use cases. It's especially useful because you can chain multiple decorators together, and thus introduce increasingly complex functionality, while still keeping each individual one of them small and focused on doing only one thing. Finally, we discussed some best practices around working with command and query handlers. First, put command and query handlers inside their respective commands and handlers; and second, don't reuse command handlers; extract similar code to domain classes, and reuse those instead. In the next module, we will talk about Simplifying the Read Model. Stay tuned.

Module 6 : Simplifying the Read Model

Introduction

In the previous modules, we created explicit commands, queries, and handlers for them.

We also introduced decorators on top of the handlers. All this allowed us to keep the code simple and maintainable, even after we faced more requirements from the stakeholders, such as the database retry behavior and audit logging. That was one of the three benefits(Simplicity, Performance, Scalability) the CQRS pattern provides, code simplicity. It is very important, probably the most important benefit, but it's not the only one CQRS provides us with. In this module, we will be exploring the Read model in the attempts to simplify it. I will show how it allows us to increase the application performance.

The State of the Read Model

Before we start the deep dive into the Read model, let me give you a refresher on the terminology.
- Command model
  - Write model
  - Write side
  - Command side
  - Writes
- Query model
  - Read model
  - Read side
  - Query side
  - Reads

The CQRS pattern is about creation of two different models, one for commands and the other one for queries. The term Query model is the same as Read model, Read side, Query side, or just Reads. And the same is true for commands. The term Command model has the same set of synonyms; Write model, Write side, Command side, or just Writes. They are all about describing the two sides of the application in CQRS. So, when we'll be talking about the Read model in this module, just keep in mind that it's the same concept as Query model. Alright, having that out of the way, let's take a look at our Read model. It currently consists of only one query, GetListQuery. It asks our application about the students who are registered in the system, and it also allows for filtering them by a particular course, or a particular number of such courses. And the handler. What it does is it calls the StudentRepository, gets a list of student entities out of it, and converts them into DTOs. Let's also look at the repository.

```
public class StudentRepository {
    @Autowired
    private UnitOfWork unitOfWork;
    public List<Student> getList(String enrolledIn, int numberOfCourses){
    Queryable<Student> query = unitOfWork.query<Student>();
    if (!enrolledIn.isEmpty()){
        query = query.Where(x => x.enrollments.any(e => e.getCourse().getName() == enrolledIn));
    }
    List<Student> result = query.toList();
    if (numberOfCourses != null){
        result = result.Where(x => x.getEnrollments().size() == numberOfCourses).toList();
    }
    return result;
  }
}
```

We have gone over it already in the past module, but let's reiterate real quick. There are some limitations. For example, you cannot use it to filter an object by the number of elements in one of its collections. You can see that we delegate the filtration by the course name to orm. That's something that orm can take care of, but when it comes to filtering the students by the number of their enrollments, the ORM cannot help us with that. It doesn't know how to transform such a filtration into a SQL query. This allows us to load partially filtered objects into memory and then complete the filtration there, which just loops through all those in-memory objects. As you might guess, because of this limitation, the performance characteristics of the GetList method are not very good. Because we cannot delegate the filtration to the database, we transfer an excessive amount of data to the application server from the database when we retrieve a not fully filtered set of students. The second issue here is the N+1 problem. In order to complete the filtration in the memory, the ORM needs the rest of the student data, particularly this Enrollments collection. Because this collection is not loaded as part of the student set, they are loaded lazily one by one. when java iterates through this collection in the memory. All this affects the performance quite badly. It's not noticeable here, of course, but in applications with high performance requirements and with large or even moderate amounts of data, that will be a problem.

Separation of the Domain Model

So, our Read model lacks the performance. How can we fix this? Well, that's what CQRS is all about. Remember, the core principle of CQRS is to have two models instead of just one. One model for Writes commands, and the other one for Reads queries. And that, in turn, allows you to optimize decisions for different situations. During the refactoring of our sample project, we have been gradually introducing this separation. Remember we had a single giant update method in the beginning of this course. We separated it into several task-based API endpoints. That was a segregation at the API level. After that, we introduced further separation when we defined explicit commands and queries and the handlers for them. Thus the split has penetrated into the Application Services layer, but even that is not enough. We need to go further and introduce the separation at the Domain model level as well. Look at the repository once again. The GetList method uses the same Domain model as the command handlers. It uses the same student entity, and that puts a restriction on what we can do with this method. As I said previously, orm doesn't provide enough functionality for us to fully utilize our database. The resulting SQL query is not optimal. So the use of the domain model limits our ability to write high-performant SQL queries, but it's also true the other way around. If you look at the GetList query handler in convertToDtos method, you can see that we are using these FirstEnrollment and SecondEnrollment properties, and if you look at the usages of them, this GetListQuery handler is the only place where they are being used. So what we have here is unnecessary over-complication of the domain model in order to fit the needs of the query side of our application. This is a very important point, so let me repeat it once again.

- Same domain model for reads and writes
    - Domain model overcomplication
    - Bad query performance

The fact that we are using the same domain model for both command and query sides of our application leads to two things. First, it overcomplicates that domain model. The domain model becomes more complex than it would otherwise; and second, it hinders our ability to fully utilize our database. We cannot utilize highly optimized database queries in such an environment.

- A complex domain model that handles neither reads nor writes well
    - Make the difference between reads and writes explicit
    - Split the domain model

And that is a perfect illustration of what you usually end up with when trying to fit the Read and Write responsibilities into a single model. You end up having a more complex domain model that handles neither of those responsibilities well. Reads and Writes are inherently different, and the best way to address this difference is to make it explicit in the code base. We have already taken some steps towards this goal, but as I said, the current state of the separation is not enough. We need to split our domain model as well. So, what this split should look like?

- Are we going to have two domain models now?
- Take the domain model out of the read side

Are we going to have two domain models now? No, it's actually not that. It's not as much of a split as it is an extraction. We are going to take the domain model out of the Read side entirely. The Read side then will not work with any domain model whatsoever. That's another important point, so let me elaborate on it.

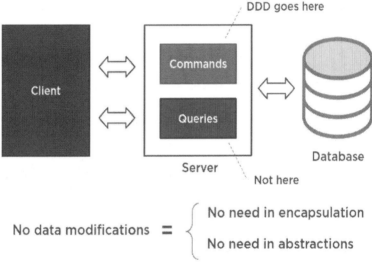

There is no need for a domain model within the Read side of the application. The domain model is only required for commands, not queries. One of the ultimate goals of domain modeling is achieving a high degree of encapsulation, making sure that when you change something in the system, all the data in it remain consistent, and no invariants are broken. But because we don't change anything on the Read side, there is no need for the encapsulation, and, by extension, no need in the domain modeling, either. The only thing the Read side needs to worry about is how to better present data to the client, and so you can just drop the domain model from the query handlers. You can get rid of all other abstractions, too. For example, you don't need an ORM here, either. You can write all the database access code manually, and that would actually be beneficial in many cases, because you would be able to use the database-specific optimization techniques that you wouldn't be able to use with a complex ORM, such as Hibernate or Entity Framework. Let's see how we can do that.

Simplifying the Read Model

Alright, we are going to get rid of the domain model entirely in the Read side of our application.
The repository . We will no longer be using reposirtory when querying data from the database. So, because we won't be using the ORM here, we don't need the SessionFactory, either. What we need instead is a direct connection to the database that we'll be running our SQL queries against. And to open such a connection, we need a connection string.

```
package logic.appServices
public class GetListQuery implements IQuery
{
public String enrolledIn;
public int numberOfCourses;
public GetListQuery(String enrolledIn, int
numberOfCourses) {
```

```java
        enrolledIn = enrolledIn;
        numberOfCourses = numberOfCourses;
}
class GetListQueryHandler implements
IQueryHandler {
    private queriesConnectionString
connectionString;
    public
GetListQueryHandler(QueriesConnectionStri
ng connectionString) {
        connectionString = connectionString;
    }
    public List<StudentDto>
handle(GetListQuery query){
            String sql = "SELECT s.StudentID
Id, s.Name, s.Email,
                s.FirstCourseName Course1,
s.FirstCourseCredits Course1Credits,
s.FirstCourseGrade Course1Grade,
                s.SecondCourseName Course2,
s.SecondCourseCredits Course2Credits,
s.SecondCourseGrade Course2Grade
            FROM dbo.Student s
            WHERE (s.FirstCourseName =
@Course
            OR s.SecondCourseName =
@Course
            OR @Course IS NULL)
                AND (s.NumberOfEnrollments =
@Number
                OR @Number IS NULL)
            ORDER BY s.StudentID ASC";

        SqlConnection connection = new
SqlConnection(connectionString.Value);
```

```
        List<StudentDto> students =
connection.query<StudentDto>(sql,
        new
GetListQuery(query.getEnrolledIn(),query.get
NumberOfCourses()).toList();
        return students;
    }
}
}
```

Alright, here is the SQL query we are going to use. No need to dive deep into it. Just note that this SQL query does everything in one database roundtrip, which greatly increases the performanceSo, here it is, our new implementation of the GetList query handler. We can now remove GetList method in the repository.

we can go to the student entity, and get rid of these two lines :

```
public Enrollment firstEnrollment =
getEnrollment(0);
public Enrollment SecondEnrollment =
getEnrollment(1);).
```

We have been using them for the sole purpose of querying the data from the database.

Recap: Simplifying the Read Model

- Simplified the read side

- Read model is a thin wrapper on top of the database
- Can use database-specific features to optimize the performance

In the previous demo, you saw how we simplified the Read side. It no longer uses the domain model, nor does it use Hibernate. We did the data retrieval manually, using a custom SQL query, and because of that, because we removed all those abstraction layers, our Read model has become just a thin wrapper on top of the database. On the one hand, it means that we now have to write all our SQL on our own, but on the other, it also means that we are not restricted by the abstraction layers. We can use as many database-specific features as we want, and that allows us to create a highly optimized and performant solution for our specific problem. Note that it's not a bad thing that the Read model is now tightly coupled to the database vendor, SQL Server in our case.

- Encapsulation

    - Data changes are consistent
    - All invariants are met

- Read side

    - No data changes

- No need in encapsulation
- No need in DDD

Remember we discussed previously in this module that one of the main goals of building a domain model is encapsulation. Making sure that any change to our data remains internally consistent, and maintains all the invariants. In the Read side of the application, we don't modify anything. Because of that, we don't have to worry about the encapsulation, and we don't have to worry about the domain modeling itself either.

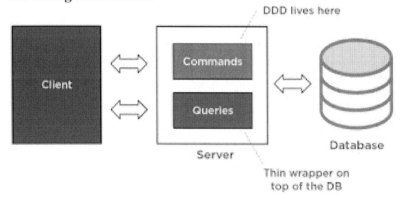

Remember, Domain-Driven Design lives on the Commands side of your application. The Read side is just a thin wrapper on top of the data storage where you can do anything you want; of course, as long as you don't modify that data. Otherwise it wouldn't be the Read side.

- Queries

- Complex SQL queries
- Vendor-specific features
- Stored procedures

You can write complex and highly optimized SQL queries. You can use vendor-specific features, such as, for example, indexed views. By the way, we could really use one of those to speed up the calculation of the number of student enrollments. Heck, you can even use stored procedures. They are usually terrible, but only if you are using them on the Write side of the application. On the Read side, they are just fine.

- Doesn't it make the read model anemic?
- There's no need in encapsulation if you don't modify any data

People often ask, doesn't such approach to the Read model make it anemic? And the answer to this question boils down to encapsulation. An anemic domain model means not encapsulated domain model. There is no need for encapsulation, if you don't modify any data. I talk about it in much more detail in my other course, Refactoring from Anemic Domain Model Towards a Rich One. Check it out for an in-depth discussion of this concern, including how anemic domain models relate to functional programming. Alright, let's go back to our recap.

- Optimized the data retrieval

- Got rid of the N+1 problem

We have optimized the data retrieval. We now select only the minimum amount of data and we do that in just one database roundtrip. In other words, we have got rid of the N+1 problem. The N+1 problem is when we first selected the students, then their enrollments, and then all their courses, all in different database roundtrips.

- ORM with enabled lazy loading leads to N+1

    - Disable lazy loading : Wroung way
    - Not use such ORMs : Wroung way
    - Don't use the ORM on the read side : Right way

That is, by the way, another common concern people have; the N+1 problem and the use of ORMs, such as Hibernate and Entity Framework. The concern boils down to the fact that it's very easy to get the N+1 problem when using an ORM with enabled lazy loading. People then sometimes go ahead and propose to either disable the lazy loading, or not even use those ORMs altogether. However, while the problem indeed exists, there is no need for such drastic measures. Just don't use the ORM or the domain model on the Read side of the application. That

would be enough to avoid the N+1 problem
and related performance issues.

- CQRS allows you to optimize, read and
  write models for the different
  requirements.

As you saw in the previous demo, the CQRS
pattern allows you to do exactly that. It allows
you to optimize each model, Read and Write
model, separately for the different
requirements our application poses to them.

```
public class Student implements  Entity {
  String name ;
  String email ;
  IList<Enrollment> enrollments = new
List<Enrollment>();
  IReadOnlyList<Enrollment> Enrollments =
enrollments.toList();
  Enrollment FirstEnrollment =
getEnrollment(0);  // removed this line
  Enrollment SecondEnrollment
=getEnrollment(1);// removed this line
}
```

- Simplified the commands side too
- The domain model focuses on
  commands only

We have also simplified the Commands side.
We have removed the FirstEnrollment and
SecondEnrollment properties that were
previously used by the GetList query. Now
our domain model focuses entirely on the
processing of commands. It exposes less state,
which is always a good thing. Also, our

repositories now have very few methods aside from GetById, Save, and Delete. That's usually all the domain model needs, when you don't use it in the Read side of the application. You can see, there is just one such method, GetByName. And in fact, we can remove these repositories altogether. There is not much value in them in our current architecture, anyway. For example, in the RegisterCommand handler, we can just remove the two repository instances, and use the UnitOfWork here directly. We have Save, GetById, and Delete methods in the UnitOfWork class already, and we can create another method called GetCourseByName here, too, to accommodate this remaining query. No need for having a whole layer with repositories that don't do much.

- It is impossible to create an optimal solution for searching, and processing of transactions utilizing a single model
- Both reads and writes benefit from the separation
- Writes benefit from removing code from the domain model that is not used for data modifications
- Reads benefit because you are able to optimize the data retrieval
- Use a "big" ORM in commands
- Use handwritten SQL in queries

Overall, this is a common pattern that I see each and every time when people start applying the CQRS pattern in their code bases. It is impossible to create an optimal solution for searching and processing of transactions utilizing a single model, and because of that, both Reads and Writes benefit from the separation. Writes benefit because you get rid of a lot of code in the domain model that is not used for data modifications, and Reads benefit because you are able to optimize the data retrieval. A common approach I recommend here is this; use a fully-fledged, highly encapsulated domain model with a big ORM such as Hibernate or Entity Framework in the commands, and use handwritten SQL with no domain model in the queries.

- 3 goals of CQRS :

  - Simplicity
  - Scalability
  - Performance

This concludes our discussion of the second goal of CQRS, performance, but before finishing this module up, let's talk about one more thing.

The Read Model and the Onion Architecture

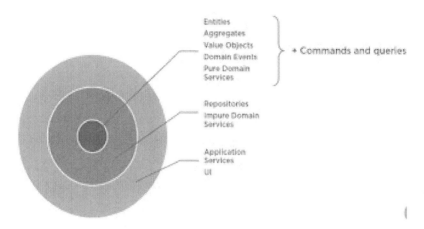

Entities
Aggregates
Value Objects
Domain Events
Pure Domain
Services
} + Commands and queries

Repositories
Impure Domain
Services

Application
Services
UI

You might have noticed a subtle inconsistency in the way we implemented the query handler in the past modules. This inconsistency relates to the onion architecture. We discussed previously that queries, just as commands and events, are part of the core domain model. They represent what the clients can ask of our application, but the same time, look at how we defined our query.

public class GetListQuery implements
IQuery<List<StudentDto>>{
String enrolledIn;
int numberOfCourses;
}

Can you see what's wrong with it? Take a moment; I'll wait a couple seconds. Ready? Okay. The problem with this query is that it implements the IQuery interface of the type List of StudentDto. Where does this

StudentDto belong on the Onion Architecture diagram?

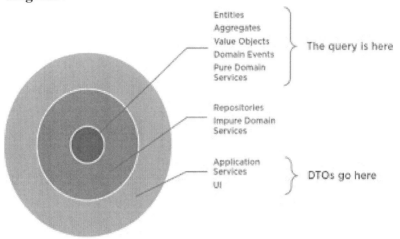

It belongs in the outermost layer of our application, because it's the data contract that we define for our clients. This DTO has nothing to do with the domain model, but we still used it from the Query, and by doing so, we have violated the domain model isolation principle. This principle states that each layer in the onion architecture, each class in that layer, can either refer to classes from the same layer or to classes from the inner layers. It cannot refer to classes that reside in layers upper in onion, but that's exactly what we are doing here.

```
public class GetListQuery implements
IQuery<List<Student>>{
String enrolledIn;
int numberOfCourses;
}
```

- **Queries no longer reside in the onion**

What we had to do instead to avoid this violation is we had to make the query return a list of students, not student DTOs, and then convert them into DTOs in the controller. This way, we would have preserved the domain model isolation. However, that's a minor issue and it's minor precisely because of what we did in this module. We no longer use the domain model in our queries. We introduced the separation on the domain model level, and because of that, our queries no longer reside in this onion. The whole domain model is now dedicated to the commands only. Queries now reside in their own Read model that is not connected to the onion architecture anymore; it's a thin wrapper on top of our database.

Summary

- Simplifying the read model

  - It no longer uses the domain model
  - Doesn't use Hibernate

- Introduced the separation at the domain model level

  - Simplified the command side
  - Optimized the query side

- The domain model no longer contains code used by the queries
- Can even get rid of repositories
- Can use database-specific features in reads

- There's no need for encapsulation in the reads
- The read model and the onion architecture

- Queries are no longer part of the onion

In this module, we discussed how to simplify the Read model. We refactored our application so that the Read side of it no longer uses the domain model. It also doesn't use Hibernate anymore. We wrote the data storage code manually, using the raw SQL. We introduced the separation at the domain model level. This separation allowed us to both simplify the command side and optimize the query side of our application. The command side has become simpler, because the domain model no longer contains the code used by the queries, and we can even get rid of the repositories entirely, as the most complex methods have migrated from them to the query handlers. This would allow us to simplify the commands even further. The query side has become optimized because we were able to use database-specific features to retrieve only the minimum amount of data, as well as do this in a single database roundtrip. In other words, the Read model has become a thin wrapper on top of the data storage. This is beneficial because there's no need for encapsulation here. The Read model doesn't mutate the data, and thus it cannot violate any invariants in the application. We also talked about the Read model and the onion architecture. There is a subtle inconsistency in how we structured our queries. It looks like they shouldn't have used the DTOs, because those DTOs belong in outer layers of the onion. However, if you consider that queries are no longer part of the onion, they are no longer part of the domain model, then the inconsistency vanishes. The only messages that remain being part of our core domain are commands and events. In the next module, we will continue exploring the Read side of our application further. We will talk about introducing a separate database for it.

Module 7 : Introducing a Separate Database for Queries

Introduction

In this module, we will talk about introducing a separate database for the queries, for the Read side of our application.

Meet Scalability

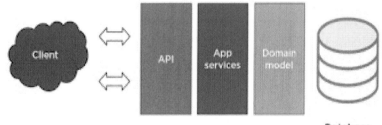

Throughout this course, we've been gradually introducing more and more separation in our application.

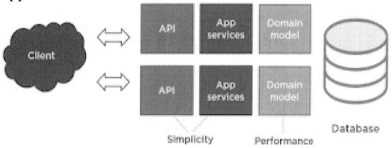

We started with splitting the API endpoints. That was a separation at the API level. Then we created explicit commands, queries and handlers for them. This way, we have split our Application Services layer. After that, we proceeded to the domain model. We have removed all references to the domain model from the Read side of our application. As we progressed with the separation, we gained more and more benefits out of it. For example, the separation at the API and the Application Services layer gave us simplicity. After extracting task-based API endpoints out of a single giant CRUD-oriented one, both our controllers and the user interface became simpler and started to make much more sense from the user perspective. Introducing explicit commands and queries allowed us to bring in the concept of decorators which, in turn, helped us implement the cross-cutting functionality with very little effort. The separation at the domain model level gave us performance. As we removed the domain model from our queries, it became much easier to optimize them, because we were no longer restricted by encapsulation and unnecessary abstractions. It also gave us additional gains in simplicity, as we were able to focus the domain model solely on command processing, and remove from it all code related to queries. As you might have guessed already, we will not be stopping here.

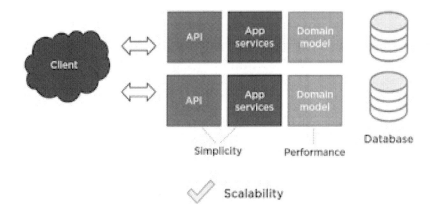

We will proceed with the separation and continue straight to the data level. We will introduce a separate database for queries, and that will provide us with the third benefit of CQRS, scalability. Let's take a minute to discuss what that is and why it is important.

- Scalability

  - Enables utilization of a number of servers

- Performance

  - Bound to a single server

So, what is scalability? It is similar to performance, but it's not the same thing. With performance optimizations, you can achieve pretty good results, but you are still bound to the resources of a single machine. There is only so much you can get out of just one server. There is a physical cap on how many resources it can provide. Scalability takes place when a single server becomes not enough. It allows you to utilize the resources of several, and potentially, an unlimited number of servers, and thus meet the demands of the ever growing user base. In a typical enterprise-level application, there's a large disparity among the operations this application handles. Among all those create, read, update, and delete operations, the one that is used the most is usually read. There are disproportionately more reads than writes in a typical system, and so it makes a lot of sense to scale them independently from each other. The separation at the data level allows you to do exactly that. Even if you still have a single server that handles all the commands, by creating a cluster of several servers just for queries, you will drastically increase the application output. Because processing of commands and queries is fundamentally asymmetrical, scaling these services asymmetrically is beneficial, too.

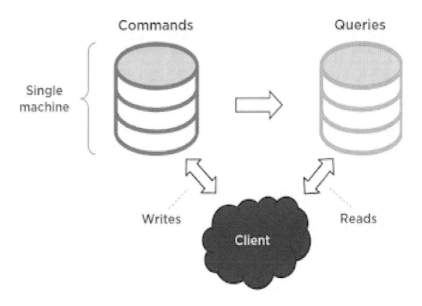

The synchronization between the databases of the command and query sides is a topic that we will discuss separately, but in general, the Commands database is a master storage for all data in the application. The Queries databases synchronize with that master storage, and then serve the reads on their own. This way, they offload the pressure from the commands. Note that although the gain in the application output is quite significant, there's still a limitation here. You are still bound to the resources of the single machine that runs the commands. CQRS by itself doesn't provide any guidance in scaling of the commands, only the queries.

- Need sharding to scale commands
- It's a rare requirement

To go even further, we would need to introduce sharding, but it's outside the scope of this book. So we won't be diving into that topic here. Keep in mind, though, that it's quite rare that a typical enterprise-level application would need to shard data in the commands, because the number of reads is usually one or even several orders of magnitude larger than the number of writes. The introduction of a separate database, or multiple databases, for reads is usually more than enough to meet all possible requirements to such an application.

Separation at the Data Level in the Real World

- Separate databases for reads and writes

  - Indexed view
  - Database replication
  - elasticsearch

We have touched upon this topic already in the first module, but it's important enough to reiterate it once again here. There are a lot of examples of this type of CQRS in the real world, where you keep separate databases for reads and writes, and you don't even necessarily need to create and maintain a separate database for that yourself. If you ever introduced an indexed view in your SQL Server, that's an example of the separation at the data level; the one that we just talked about. Here, the database server provides all the required infrastructure, and so you might not even think about it as being a form of CQRS, but it still is, nonetheless.

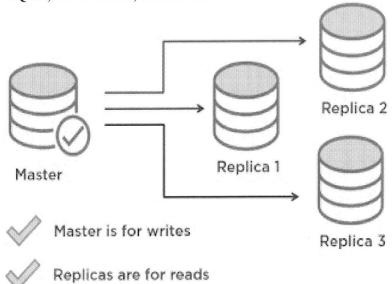

Another example is database replication, when you have one master database and several replicas that get all the updates from the master node automatically. Here, the database software also does all the work for you so that you don't need to worry about the data synchronization, but the principle is exactly the same. You have a single node that is a master of all the data in the system, and you have one or more replicas that pick up all the updates from that single node and then can be used to serve the reads. This way, they offload the pressure from the master database, and allow you to scale the overall system output. So, one master node for writes, and several replica nodes for reads. Finally, another common example is ElasticSearch. It's a full-text search engine that works by indexing data, usually from a relational database, and providing rich capabilities to query it. So you can see that, in order to achieve the third benefit, scalability, you don't necessarily need to implement the separation at the data level yourself. You can leverage an already existing software, which can be just as good, but at the same time, saves a lot of effort.

Designing a Database for Queries

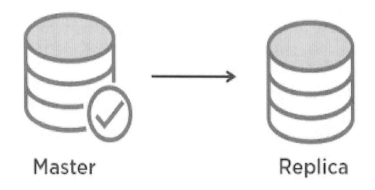

Master   Replica

 Replicas have the same structure

Database features that work out of the box can be easy to use, and you should definitely consider them first before rolling out your own implementation; however, they are quite limited in the type of functionality they provide. For example, with the out-of-the-box database replication, despite the fact that you will have separate physical databases for queries, those databases will still have the same structure, but as we know, reads and writes have very different needs, and the same database structure, just as the use of the same unified domain model, might not fit well the read side of our application.

```
SELECT s.*, e.Grade, c.Name CourseName,
c.Credits
FROM dbo.Student s
LEFT JOIN (
SELECT e.StudentID, COUNT(*) Number
FROM dbo.Enrollment e
GROUP BY e.StudentID) t ON s.StudentID =
t.StudentID
LEFT JOIN dbo.Enrollment e ON
e.StudentID = s.StudentID
LEFT JOIN dbo.Course c ON e.CourseID =
c.CourseID
WHERE (c.Name = @Course OR @Course IS
NULL)
AND (ISNULL(t.Number, 0) = @Number OR
@Number IS NULL)
ORDER BY s.StudentID ASC
```

And indeed, if you look at our SQL query, you can see that although we squeezed everything we could out of it in terms of performance, there could be done much more if we just had a more appropriate database schema. Here it is, the schema of the commands database.

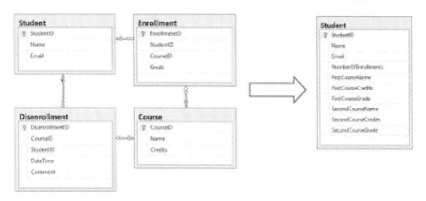

We could denormalize it into something like above. Yes, that's the whole database; just one table with this seemingly terrible structure.

- Why denormalize the queries database?

So, what's the reasoning behind such a drastic change? This database structure is a much better fit for the needs of our Read model. Here's our UI once again.

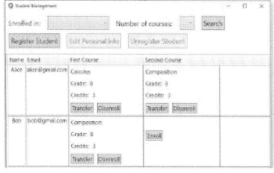

What data do we need to compose such a UI? Well, first of all, we need the students themselves, their names and emails. Then we need the information about their first and second enrollments; the name of the course, the grade, and the number of credits they will get. We can only have two enrollments currently, and we also need the total number of courses in order to support our filtration functionality here. And if you look at our new database, that's exactly the information we are having here, in the student table. It has the name and the email of the student, the total number of enrollments, which can be either zero, 1, or 2 at this point, and we have the information about the first and the second enrollments; the course name, the number of credits, and the grade. We have adjusted the schema of this database to perfectly match the needs of the Read side of our application. No need to assemble the required information with a complicated SQL query anymore. All we need is now represented by this single, flat table. And let's see how we can simplify the SQL query. Here is the old one once again.

```
SELECT s.*, e.Grade, c.Name CourseName, c.Credits
FROM dbo.Student s
LEFT JOIN (
SELECT e.StudentID, COUNT(*) Number
FROM dbo.Enrollment e
GROUP BY e.StudentID) t ON s.StudentID = t.StudentID
LEFT JOIN dbo.Enrollment e ON e.StudentID = s.StudentID
LEFT JOIN dbo.Course c ON e.CourseID = c.CourseID
WHERE (c.Name = @Course OR @Course IS NULL)
```

AND (ISNULL(t.Number, 0) = @Number OR
@Number IS NULL)
ORDER BY s.StudentID ASC
SELECT s.*
FROM dbo.Student s
WHERE (s.FirstCourseName = @Course
OR s.SecondCourseName = @Course OR
@Course IS NULL)
AND (s.NumberOfEnrollments = @Number
OR @Number IS NULL)
ORDER BY s.StudentID ASC

You can see it gathers the information from three out of four tables in the main database; student, enrollment, and course, and here is how the SQL will look should we introduce the new database, much simpler and much more concise. Again, we can do that because all the information the Read side needs resides in a single table with the schema that matches our needs perfectly. Let's see how it can look in practice.

Creating a Database for Queries

I've already created the database with the schema we discussed off-screen. Here it is, with just a single table, Student.

Student

🔑	StudentID
	Name
	Email
	NumberOfEnrollments
	FirstCourseName
	FirstCourseCredits
	FirstCourseGrade
	SecondCourseName
	SecondCourseCredits
	SecondCourseGrade

This is the table's columns, and this is the data inside. I've added a couple of rows manually off-screen as well. Alright, we now have two databases; one for reads and the other one for writes. And so we need another class to represent the this new database connection string. Let's go to our existing ConnectionString class, and add a new one, QueriesConnectionString, and rename this one to CommandsConnectionString. Note that you could just add another field in the already existing ConnectionString class, so that it would contain information about the both databases, but that would be a violation of the interface segregation principle; the I letter among the SOLID principles. That's because you never actually need both of them. You don't need to create connections to both databases at the same time. It's also much less error prone to have two classes instead of just one. This way, you will not be able to accidentally mistake one for the other. For example, pass a connection string for queries where the connection string for commands is required. Okay, now we need to add the actual connection string, the string itself. That would be our config file. I am naming it QueriesConnectionString, and specifying the database name. We need to turn the old ConnectionString into the CommandsConnectionString. That's because we will be using our ORM only in the Commands side of the application, and in the query handler, we need to accept a QueriesConnectionString. Note that the Read and Write databases are not synchronized yet. So if we try to update, say, Alice's personal info, it will not be displayed here, but hey, one step at a time.

Recap: Creating a Database for Queries

- Created a separate database for queries and re-targeted the query handler

In the previous demo, you saw how we created a separate database for queries and re-targeted the query handler to work with it instead of the commands database. As a result, we were able to significantly simplify the query handler.

```
public List<StudentDto>
handle(GetListQuery query) {
```

```
string sql = "SELECT * FROM dbo.Student
s
WHERE (s.FirstCourseName = @Course
OR s.SecondCourseName = @Course
OR @Course IS NULL)
AND (s.NumberOfEnrollments = @Number
OR @Number IS NULL)
ORDER BY s.StudentID ASC";
SqlConnection connection = new
SqlConnection(connectionString.getValue())) {
List<StudentDto> students = connection
.query<StudentDto>(sql,
  new
GetListQuery(query.getEnrolledIn(),query.get
NumberOfCourses())
).toList();
return students;
}
```

As you can see, it now consists of just the SQL query itself, which we also simplified quite significantly, and it also consists of the single call to the database. We didn't even have to transform the data from the database using the private class as a temporary data storage. We rendered the results directly to the DTO. All this is a result of designing the new database in a way that perfectly aligns with the needs of our read model. As I mentioned previously, Read and Write models have different requirements, and it's impossible to come up with a single approach that would fit both of them.

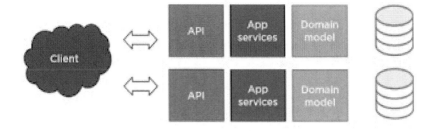

 Applied different architectural approaches to the read and write models

The only way we can fulfill the needs of both the Read and the Write models is if we apply different architectural approaches to them, and we did exactly that.

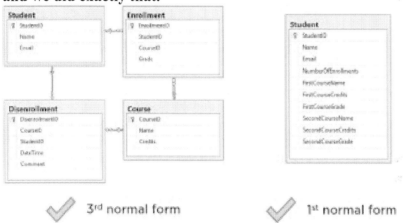

3ʳᵈ normal form   1ˢᵗ normal form

Our database for commands complies with the third normal form, which is good for transaction processing. Whereas the database for reads is denormalized. The denormalization allowed us to minimize the number of joins and the amount of post-processing needed to get a given set of data. In fact, we didn't have any joins and any post-processing whatsoever.

- High normal forms are good for commands; low normal forms are good for queries.

Note that it's a common phenomena in a lot of enterprise-level applications. High normal forms are good for commands and low normal forms are good for queries. We could go even further with the database for reads and introduce a different type of data storage, such as a document database. You need to look at what works best for the requirements you have for your Read model.

Scalability

Alright, these are all the first and the second benefits of CQRS, code simplicity and performance. How about scalability, the third one? Where is it in our code base?

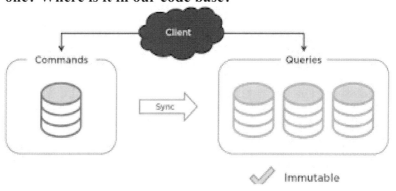

Now that we have separated our database into two data storages, it's easy to scale the Read side of the application. Just create as many databases for reads as you need, and make them synchronize with the database for writes. We will be talking about the synchronization strategies in the next module, but you need to implement this process only once. After that, you will be able to use it for as many databases as you would like. That's because of the immutable nature of the Read model. It doesn't mutate any state, it doesn't leave any side effects, and so it can be scaled pretty much indefinitely. It's not as simple to implement scaling within the command model, precisely because there's data mutation involved, but in the Read model, it is simple.

- Application

  - Write model
  - Read model : Web client
  - Read model 2 : Mobile client

Note that in our application, we are having just one Read model, but you could need more than one and thus, you could need to create more than one database with its own schema and synchronization mechanism. An example here is a mobile versus a web client. A mobile client usually doesn't need as much data as a web one, and it also could need it in another format. So it might make sense to create separate read models for each of them, and adjust those Read models to align perfectly with the clients' needs. Of course, if the needs of these two clients are not as different, then the single Read model would do just fine. So evaluate each different situation separately to see what makes the most sense in your particular case.

A Word of Caution Regarding the Database for Reads

- Be prudent when applying the CQRS pattern

A word of caution, though. You need to be prudent when applying software design patterns, including the CQRS pattern. There are costs and benefits attached to any design decision, and you need to carefully consider them before implementing it. Up to the point where you separate everything except the data storage, the maintainability costs of such a separation are not that high, and in most typical enterprise-level applications, the benefits will greatly overweight the costs. However, the situation changes when you introduce a new database to the mix, the database for Reads. The synchronization between the two databases introduces quite a lot of complexity. Eventual consistency between them, which we'll talk about in the next module, also introduces potential confusion for the users. For example, if you register a new student, and this student doesn't appear in the Read database right away, that might confuse your users, to the point when they might decide to register the student again and will end up having two same student records. You can mitigate this confusion by showing some information on the UI, for example, a message that the student is sent to the system and will be processed within a minute or two, but still, you need to be careful here.

- Eventual consistency and maintaining a separate database are significant costs

  - In most cases, you are just fine without a separate database for reads
  - CQRS can be just as effective with a only a single database.

Eventual consistency, plus the additional effort of maintaining a separate database, add up to being quite significant costs, and in most cases, you would be just fine without a separate database for reads. The CQRS pattern can be just as effective with only a single database. Having that said, if you do need to scale your system, particularly the Read side of it, then a separate database can be a great solution for you.

Summary

- Introduced a separate database for queries

- Completed implementing the CQRS pattern
- Reads and writes are separated at each level: API, app services, domain model, DB
- Adjusted the read database for the needs of the query model
- Can scale the reads indefinitely

- Scalability: utilizing the resources of more than one server
- Examples of the separation at the data level:

  - Indexed views
  - Database replication
  - ElasticSearch

- Designed the database for reads

  - Denormalized and thus adjusted it to the needs of the read model
  - Minimized the number of joins and the amount of post-processing

- The 3rd normal relational form is for commands; the 1st form for queries
- Might need a separate read database for each client
- Maintaining the synchronization is costly; eventual consistency is confusing

- In many cases, a single database is enough

In this module, we've introduced a separate database for Reads. This way, we have completed implementing the CQRS pattern. Now the Read and Write models are separated at each level; the API, the Application Services layer, the domain model, and the data storage. This separation allowed us to adjust the Read database perfectly for the needs of our query model, and thus simplify that model. And it also allowed us to scale the reads. Now we can have as many copies of the Read database as we need, and thus scale this part of our application pretty much indefinitely. We talked about what scalability is. This characteristic is similar to performance, but it's not the same thing. With performance optimizations, you are still bound to the resources of a single machine. Scalability means that you can utilize the resources of several and, potentially, an unlimited number of servers. There are plenty of examples of such a database level separations in the real world; indexed views, database replication, ElasticSearch are all examples of CQRS to some degree. You saw how we designed the database for reads. We have adjusted it to the needs of our Read model by denormalizing it. We had only one table in that database that contained all information about the students; their personal data, and both courses they are enrolled in. This allowed us to minimize the number of

161

joins and the amount of post-processing we needed to get a given set of data. You will end up with this pattern in most applications; third normal relational form for the commands database, and the first form for the queries one. We discussed that you might want to have separate Read models, and by extension, separate read databases, for each client of your application, such as mobile and web. And we also discussed that you need to be cautious when introducing the second database. The additional costs associated with synchronization between the databases, and the potential confusion the eventual consistency introduces, might not be worth the benefits you get out of it. In many cases, a single database would be enough. Only introduce the second database if you truly need to scale your application. In the next module, we will talk about synchronizing the commands and queries databases. We will discuss different strategies of such a synchronization, and we will also talk about eventual consistency and the CAP theorem in the context of CQRS.

Module 8 : Synchronizing the Commands and Queries Databases

Introduction

- Synchronization -> Eventual consistency -> The CAP theorem

In this module, we will talk about synchronizing the commands and queries databases. We will also discuss eventual consistency and the CAP theorem in the context of CQRS.

State-driven Projections

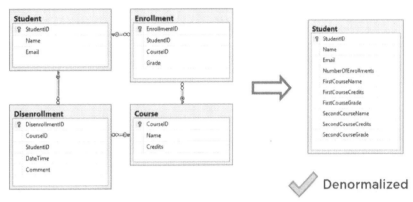

✓ Denormalized

 Need a projection

In the previous module, we introduced a new database for the Read part of our application. This new database is perfectly aligned with the needs of our queries. It is denormalized, and consists of only one table. The fact that there are now two separate databases means there should be a synchronization between them; such a synchronization is also called projection. So keep in mind that the words synchronization and projection are synonyms in the context of CQRS.

- Projections :
    - Event-driven
    - State-driven
        - Sync
        - Async

So, let's talk about what strategies we could employ to implement such a projection. Those strategies can be divided into two categories, by the type of triggers that drive them. First, it is the projection driven by state, and second, the projection driven by events. The projection driven by state, in turn, can be divided into two sub-categories, synchronous and asynchronous. Let's take this first category, projections driven by state. It kind of sounds fancy, but it's really simple.

- State-driven projections
  - Flags in data tables
    - A flag per each aggregate

The idea behind it is that you have a flag in each aggregate's table that tells you the aggregate has been updated since the last synchronization, and you need to synchronize it once again.

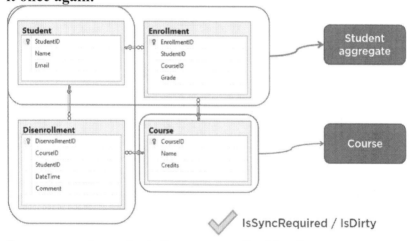

IsSyncRequired / IsDirty

In our sample project, the commands side of the application contains two aggregates, Student and Course. And so you wouldn't need to add four new columns, one for each table, but rather just two, one for the Student table, and the other one for the Course table. You can call it IsSyncRequired, IsDirty, or something similar.

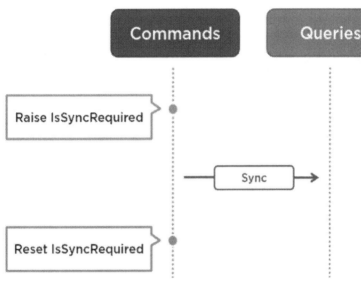

So, whenever a student gets updated, and that includes the data in the student, enrollment, and disenrollment tables; whenever they get updated, you raise the IsSyncRequired flag in the Student table. A separate synchronization process that runs at background then picks it up and either inserts a new row into the Read database, or updates an existing one. After that, it resets the flag.

Synchronization

- Offloads the pressure

You can also add a separate small table, named Synchronization, with another flag in it called IsSyncRequired. This table will have just one row. Whenever any flag in the database is raised, the flag in that small table will be raised as well. The reason for this separate table is that the background synchronization process will be sampling changes in the commands database pretty often, and may potentially put a lot of pressure on the Student and the Course tables. The additional table will allow you to offload that pressure. Now the synchronization process will be sampling just this one table, instead of all students and courses. It will query the students and courses, only if the flag in the synchronization table is set to true.

- State-driven projection
  - Straightforward
  - Easy to use
- To rebuild the read database, raise the flag for all records

This projection mechanism is very straightforward, simple, and also easy to use. If you would ever need to rebuild the Read database, you just need to raise the flag for all records. And you can do that selectively, too, for just a subset of records.

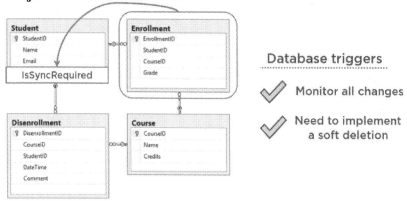

There are two ways to implement the commands part of this mechanism, the part that is responsible for raising the IsSyncRequired flags. First, create a database trigger. This trigger would monitor changes in all of your database tables, and update the flags accordingly. For example, if we enroll

167

Alice in a new course, a new enrollment row will be inserted. The trigger can interpret this insertion as an update of the corresponding student, and can raise the flag for Alice's record, as well as the flag in the Synchronization table to let the background synchronization process do its job. Note that in order to handle the deletion, you would need to modify the way you handle unregistering of students. Instead of actually deleting them, you would need to implement a soft deletion with an IsDeleted flag. Then the deletion of a record will be treated the same way as a modification of it.

- Introduce the flags in the domain model
    - Add a flag to Student and Course

The second way to raise a flag is to introduce it in the domain model itself explicitly, instead of relying on a database trigger. You can add two new IsSyncRequired properties to the domain model, one in the Student entity, and the other one in the course one, and update those properties whenever the client code modifies anything in those aggregates. That's pretty easy to do if your domain model is encapsulated. Here is an example.

```
public class Student implemets  Entity {
private String name;
private String email;
private boolean isSyncRequired;
//getters & setters
public void removeEnrollment(Enrollment enrollment, String comment) {
```

```
enrollments.remove(enrollment);
Disenrollment disenrollment = new
Disenrollment(enrollment.getStudent(),
enrollment.getCourse(), comment);
disenrollments.add(disenrollment);
isSyncRequired = true;
}
}
```

- Event listeners in Hibernate
- Change tracker in Entity Framework

You can see that when we remove an enrollment, we raise the IsSyncRequired flag, too. And of course, to make this work, you would need to override the setters of the name and the email properties so that whenever the client code assigns a new value to them, the flag is raised as well. To raise the flag in the separate Synchronization table, you can use Event listeners in NHibernate or the Change Tracker in Entity Framework. This way, whenever you see an entity is being persisted with the IsSyncRequired flag, you will be able to automatically raise the flag in the Synchronization table, too.

- Database triggers   VS   Explicit flags in the domain model
  - Choose triggers only if you don't control the source code
  - Choose the explicit implementation by default

So, which one of these two ways to raise the flag should you choose? The one with the trigger or the one with the flags in the domain model? If you have control over the domain model, then go the explicit route, with the

169

explicit flags in the domain model. It's always better to be explicit about what you do in the code. It tremendously improves the maintainability of your code base. Choose the approach with the database triggers, only if you don't have other choice; for example when you don't have control over your domain model.

Synchronous State-driven Projections

- Projections :
  - Event-driven
  - State-driven
    - Sync
    - Async

That was an example of an asynchronous state-driven projection strategy. The projection is driven by the state of the database, particularly the IsSyncRequired flags in it, and there is a separate background process that does the actual projection. It monitors those flags, and rebuilds the query database if it sees any changes.

- Sync
  - Runs synchronously
- Async
  - Runs asynchronously
- Asynchronous = Without blocking
- Application doesn't wait for the sync job

Let's now look at synchronous state-driven projection strategies. The difference between them, as you can guess from their names, is that one of them runs synchronously, and the other one asynchronously. So, what that means, exactly? The word asynchronous means without blocking the main worker. In the examples we discussed previously, the application is able to update a student in the database and continue working. A separate process then picks up this modification and does the projection. Our application doesn't wait for that separate process to complete this job, and so we can say that the projection is done asynchronously.

- Synchronous version
  - Application does the projection
  - Increases the processing time
  - All changes are immediately consistent

So, how the synchronous version would look then? The synchronous version is when the application itself does all the work or waits until the background process completes the projection before returning an OK to the client. This approach is rarely applied when you have two separate databases for reads and writes, mainly because it increases the processing times quite dramatically. However, the benefit here is that the Read and the Write models are immediately consistent, which eliminates this confusion from the users when they don't see their changes immediately after submitting them. It might be very helpful if this is a strong requirement from your customer. I wouldn't recommend that you normally do that, though, at least not when there are two separate databases for commands and queries. Either implement the projection asynchronously, or keep the Read and Write models in the same database, to decrease the latency.

- Synchronous projections don't scale

Because of the additional latency, the synchronous projections don't scale well. That's because the latency will increase each time you add a new database copy for the queries. Your main application will have to update all the Read databases on its own, each time it modifies anything in the commands database, and the more databases you introduce for the reads, the more time it will take your application to update them all.

- Sync
  - Indexed views
- Async
  - Database replication

There are two common examples of the state-driven projection strategies. Indexed views is an example of a synchronous projection. That's because all indexed views in relational databases are updated immediately, along with the tables they derive their data from. An example of an asynchronous projection is database replication. Database replicas, unlike the indexes views, are updated asynchronously.

Event-driven Projections

- Event-driven projections
  - Domain events drive the changes
  - Subscribe to domain events

Another category of projections is event-driven projection. The main differentiating factor here is that event-driven projections are not driven by state, but instead they are driven by domain events. So, instead of the

IsSyncRequired flags, and instead of the separate Synchronization table, the projection process will subscribe to the domain events the command side raises, and will use the information from those events to update the Read database.

- Event-driven projections
  - Scales really well
  - Can use a message bus
  - Cannot rebuild the read database

The benefit of this approach is that it scales really well, even better than the approach with asynchronous state-driven projections. That's because your application can just publish the domain events on a message bus, and you can have as many projection processes subscribing to those events as you want. They will not put additional pressure on the commands database. However, there's a significant drawback to this approach. There is no easy way to rebuild the Read database from scratch or re-run the projection in case of an error.

- State
  - Don't store domain events
  - Impossible to derive events from state
- Transition to event sourcing

In our commands database, the source of all data is the state, the current state of the students and the courses. We don't store the domain events that led to that state, and because it's impossible to derive the domain events from the latest state, your Read databases will become out of sync should they miss any domain event for some reason. You could mitigate this issue by storing the domain events along with the state in the commands database, but that would be quite a significant complexity overhead. And really, if you are going to store the domain events in the database anyway, then you should probably transition to an event-sourced architecture. Event sourcing is outside the scope of this book, though.

- How should you choose the projection type?
- Without event sourcing
  - State-driven projection
- With event sourcing
  - Event-driven projection
- Align the projection strategy with the persistence mechanism

So, the rule of thumb here is this. If you are implementing the CQRS pattern without event sourcing, that is, you don't store the domain events in your commands database, and just persist the latest state instead, then don't employ the event-driven projection approach. The state-driven projections would be a much better fit for you. On the other hand, if you are using event sourcing where the domain events are the first-class citizens in your database, then of course, use the event-driven projections. In this case, you will be able to rebuild the Read database by re-raising all the events in your commands database. In other words, align the projection strategies with the type of persistence mechanism you have chosen for your project.

Consistency

- Having two databases instead of one introduces latency

- May end up with duplicate records
- You will still gain a lot of benefits even with a single database

We discussed in the previous module that having two databases instead of one, introduces latency between the Write and the Read models. It brings in a potential confusion for the users, and you should carefully consider this drawback. For example, after registering a student, the user might not see the that new student immediately, decide that they did something wrong, register that student again, and end up with having two identical student records. If your customer strongly opposes such a user experience, then just go with the single database for reads and writes. You will still gain most of the benefits of the CQRS pattern. However, if your customer is not opposed to relaxing the consistency requirements, there are some ways to mitigate this potentially confusing experience.

- Ways to mitigate the potential confusion
  - Uniqueness constraints
  - Commands database is always immediately consistent

First of all, in many cases, there will be uniqueness constraints on most of the data in the commands database, and that will help avoid the duplicates. For example, there might be a requirement that all students' email addresses must be unique. In this case, even if the user doesn't see the new student right away, and try to register them again, the system will return an error saying that such student is already registered. Note that the consistency issues only involve the queries database. The commands database is always immediately consistent, and because you run the uniqueness constraint validations against the commands database, there will be no duplicates and the user will receive a proper error message. Let's actually elaborate on this point.

- How should you query the database during a command execution?
  - Run a query from a command handler?
  - Queries database might not be up to date with the commands database

People often ask, what if I need to query the database during a command execution, for example, to check for the email uniqueness constraint, and should I run a query from a command handler to do that? And the answer is, no. You shouldn't use a query for that, because the queries work with their own database, that might not be up to date with the commands database.

- Query the commands database

In order to verify that the email is unique, you can query the data storage, but that should be the commands data storage, because it's always up to date. Just use a regular repository or the UnitOfWork class for that.

- Reading read the commands database
  - Part of the command processing flow
  - Results don't cross the application boundaries
- Reading read the queries database

So, you will still need to read the database from your commands. The difference between such reads and what the queries do is that the reads the commands perform are part of the command processing flow. The results of those reads don't cross the boundaries of the application. In other words, they are not intended for the user. Remember. after finishing the full separation between commands and queries in the previous module, we still had some read operations remaining in the repositories.

```
public class StudentRepository{
   public Student getById(long id){
      return unitOfWork.get<Student>(id);
   }
}
public class CourseRepository{
   public Course getByName(String name){
      return
unitOfWork.query<Course>().singleOrDefaul
t(x ->    x.Name == name);
   }
}
```

- Serve the commands, not queries

That's the read operations I'm talking about; GetStudentById, GetCourseByName, and potentially GetStudentByEmail. They are intended to serve the commands, not queries.

- You are not able to efficiently query the current state with Event Sourcing
- Have to query the read database

Note that it's a different story if you are implementing event sourcing. In this case, you are not able to efficiently query the current state from the commands database, because your database stores events, not the state, and so you will need to query the Read database in this case. You won't have any other choice, and you will have to deal with inconsistencies that flow from that. That's a whole other topic, though, and it should be addressed in another book. We will not be diving into it here.

Eventual Consistency

- Train users not to expect data to be immediately consistent
- Wouldn't the software become less usable without immediate consistency?

Alright, so uniqueness validations are one way to mitigate the issues with the consistency. Another way to do that is to train your users not to expect the data they see on the screen to be immediately consistent. I know, that sounds like cheating, and it looks like it just shifts the burden from lazy programmers to the users. After all, the software will become less usable if the users wouldn't see the results of their actions immediately, right? Actually, no. While it might be plausible to think that the users expect immediate consistency all the time, in reality, they don't.

- The concept of immediate consistency is counterintuitive

In fact, the whole concept of immediate consistency is counter-intuitive, because it's not how the things work in the real world. Think about it.

- Driver's license
  - Are changes in the real world immediately consistent?
  - The real world is inherently asynchronous and eventually consistent
  - Users quickly learn the concept of eventual consistency

178

When you move to a new home, do you expect your driver's license to reflect this change immediately? Of course, not. Your driver's license will show the old address until you go to a DMV, and ask them to issue a replacement. And during this quite long period of time, the information on your current driver's license will remain stale; it will remain obsolete. All your interactions with the real world are inherently asynchronous and involve eventual consistency, and the world around us is eventually consistent, too. Heck, even physics itself it eventually consistent. The information in the universe is passed with the speed of light, which is quite fast, but it's still not instantaneous. And so it doesn't take your users much effort to learn the concept of eventual consistency, because they already experience it in the real world, and in fact, it's the concept of immediate consistency that they learn when they start working with computers, not the other way around. You have probably already understood what eventual consistency stands for, but let me give an official definition. Eventual consistency is a consistency model, which guarantees that if no new updates are made to a given data item, eventually all accesses to that item will return the last updated value. So, in our example with the commands and queries databases, it means that if we modify a student, this change will eventually propagate to the Read database, and our users will be able see it on the UI.

- Display helpful messages and set proper expectations

You can foster the user acceptance of the eventual consistency by displaying helpful messages and setting proper expectations.

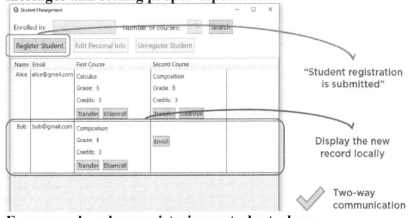

"Student registration is submitted"

Display the new record locally

Two-way communication

For example, when registering a student, show a text message saying that the student registration is submitted and will be processed shortly. This way the user will understand that this process takes time, and they shouldn't expect it to be completed immediately. Another way to handle this it to trick your users. Whenever they register a student, do update the student list, but do that locally, on the user machine only. By the time they refresh their screen again, this student will already be in the queries database, and the query result will contain the latest data. You can go even further and implement a two-way communication between the UI and the Read model. So, whenever the Read model receives an update, it will send a message to the UI with the updated search results. That would add some complexity, though, because you will need to keep the connection between the UI and the backend open, and it most cases, a simple message or the trick with the local data update would be enough.

- Separate database for reads →>
  Eventual Consistency
  - Starbucks doesn't use two-phase
    commit

So, to summarize, if you decide to introduce a separate database for reads, then your query side will not be immediately consistent. It will be eventually consistent, which might or might not be acceptable, depending on the requirements your stakeholders pose to your application. There is a great article about how consistency is handled in the real world, called Starbucks Doesn't Use Two-Phase Commit.

Versioning

- Eventual consistency is problematic
  when the cost of making a decision
  based on the stale data is high.

There could be one area where the eventual consistency is problematic, and that is when you need to make a decision based on the current data, and the cost of making that decision based on the stale data is very high. This is almost never the case, though. One of the few exceptions here is high-frequency stock trading. In all other cases, you can mitigate this problem with versioning. You can keep a version of an aggregate in both the Read and Write databases, and then if you see that the user tries to update the stale record, show them an error. This is called optimistic concurrency control. Here's an example.

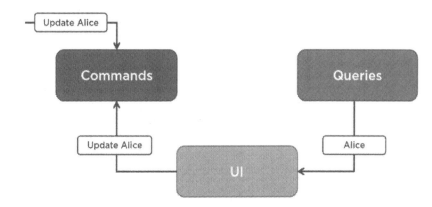

✓ Make the version number part
of all the communications

Let's say that you are requesting a list of
students from the Read database, and it
returns you Alice's record with version one.
Let's also say that someone updates Alice's
personal information, and so the version of
her record in the commands database
becomes two. Then you also try to update her
personal information based on the stale data
from the queries database. In order to
mitigate this issue, you just need to make this
version number part of all the
communications between the UI, the
command, and the Read models.

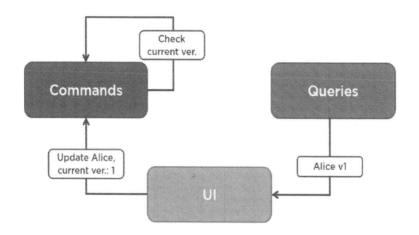

Make the version number part of all the communications

So, when the UI queries the Read model, it receives the version number, and includes it in the command that it sends to the Write model. The Write model can compare the version number in the command with the current version number of the aggregate and, if they are different, it can raise a concurrency error and reject the change. This way, you will inform the user that they need to refresh their screen to see the latest updates and include them into their new update request.

CQRS and the CAP Theorem

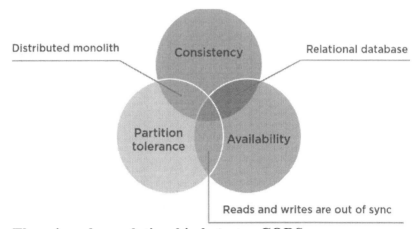

There is a close relationship between CQRS and the CAP theorem. The CAP theorem states that it is impossible for a distributed data store to simultaneously provide more than two out of the following three guarantees: consistency, availability, and partition tolerance. Consistency means that every read receives the most recent write or an error. Availability, that every request receives a response, part from outages that affect all nodes in the system; and partition tolerance, that the system continues to operate despite messages being dropped, or delayed, between the network nodes. For example, if you choose availability and consistency, that would be a typical relational database server running on a single node. All read requests to this server always get the latest version of the data, and this server is always available. The drawback here is that there is no partition tolerance, meaning that you cannot have more than one server working for your application. If you choose consistency and partition tolerance, that would be an anti-pattern called distributed monolith. All reads to such a system will still be fully consistent with the writes, but because you also chose partition tolerance, there are now multiple servers, and to ensure the consistency among all of them, you will need to block the whole system, and wait until each change propagates to every server. This would make the system unresponsive and unavailable for the period of time during which it waits for the propagation to complete. Imagine what would happen if when you post a picture on Facebook, the whole website would stop working to ensure that your friends' newsfeed is consistent with your latest update. And finally, if you choose availability and partition tolerance, then you do that at the expense of consistency, which means that if there is a connectivity loss between two servers, and you allow them to work independently, then they can go out of sync with each other really quickly. So, again, you can pick two out of the three guarantees, but you can never pick all three, which means that you need to find a proper balance for your particular situation.

- Finding a proper balance is hard
    - CQRS allows you to make different choices for reads and writes

CQRS is great, because it allows you to make different choices for reads and writes.

- Writes
    - Full consistency
    - Give up partition tolerance
- Reads
    - Give up full consistency
    - Partitionability

The trick here is to make the trade-off between partitioning and consistency differently on the Read and Write sides. In most cases, you can give full consistency on the commands side, and give up a level of partition tolerance. That's the typical relation database server scenario. You can do that as long as all your command handlers can operate on a single machine. At the same time, you can give up the full consistency on the queries side in order to obtain partitionability. You want to ensure partitionability on the Read side, because you want to scale the reads up to several machines to enable scalability. And you want to ensure consistency on the Write side, to make sure all changes are consistent, at the expense of having only one machine that handles the commands.

Summary

- **Synchronization between commands and queries**
- **State-driven projection**
    - **Introducing an IsSyncRequired flag in aggregates**
    - **Database triggers or explicit in the model update**
    - **Choose the explicit route by default**
    - **Synchronous and asynchronous**
- **Event-driven projection**
    - **Using domain events to build the queries database**
- **Without Event Sourcing: use state-driven projections**

- With Event Sourcing: use event-driven projections
- Immediate vs. eventual consistency
  - Immediate consistency is contrary to the real world experience
  - People pick up eventual consistency quickly
  - Implement data versioning and the optimistic concurrency control
- CAP theorem
  - CQRS is about making different choices with regards to the balance within CAP
  - Choose consistency and availability at the expense of partitioning for writes
  - Choose availability and partitioning at the expense of consistency for reads

In this module, we discussed the synchronization between the commands and queries databases. Such synchronization is also called projection. You learned about the two projection strategies, using state versus using events as the drivers for it. State-driven projection is when you introduce an IsSyncRequired flag in the aggregates' tables, and raise it whenever there's a change to them. You can use this flag using database triggers, or explicitly in your domain model. The explicit route is the better choice in most cases. The state-driven projections can be synchronous and asynchronous. Synchronous projections don't scale well, so choose the asynchronous option by default. We also discussed event-driven projections. That is, when you use the domain events raised by the commands side to build the queries database. The rule of thumb here is this. If you are implementing the CQRS pattern without event-sourcing, that is, if you persist the state, then use the state-driven projection. If you persist events instead of state, then choose the event-driven one. We talked about immediate and eventual consistency. Although you might be used to immediate consistency in the world of relational databases, that's not how the real world operates, and people usually don't have trouble dealing with eventual consistency in the software, too; just set proper expectations, and implement data versioning to enable the optimistic concurrency control. Finally, we discussed the CAP theorem in the context of CQRS. Remember, CQRS is about making different choices for different situations, particularly for Read and Write sides of your application. And that is also true when it comes to finding the balance within the CAP theorem. Choose consistency and availability at the expense of partitioning for writes, and choose availability and partitioning at the expense of consistency for reads. In the next module, we will talk about CQRS Best Practices and Common Misconceptions.

Module 9 : CQRS Best Practices and Misconceptions

Introduction

In this module, we will talk about some of the best practices and common misconceptions around the CQRS pattern.

CQRS and Event Sourcing

- CQRS   ?   Event Sourcing

We have come a long way refactoring our application to follow the CQRS pattern. Let's reiterate some of the best practices and misconceptions we encountered along the way, as well as discuss some that we haven't yet talked about. The first one is the relation between CQRS and Event Sourcing.

- No segregation   →>   CQRS
  →>   Event Sourcing

CQRS is often described as a stepping stone to Event Sourcing. In other words, it's described as just a transition stage that eventually leads to the Event Sourced architecture. It is not the case.

- CQRS can provide a lot of benefits without Event Sourcing.

CQRS can be applied on its own, and may provide a lot of benefits to the project, even if you never implement Event Sourcing.

- The bar for Event Sourcing is much higher than it is for CQRS
- There's still a lot of value in event sourced systems

Even more, Event Sourcing brings a lot of complexity to the table, and the bar for it is much higher than it is for CQRS; even higher than for the separation at the database level that we discussed in the two previous modules. Having that said, there is still a lot of value in event sourced systems, too; it's just the complexity overhead is not as often justified as for CQRS.

- Finance tech
  - Has to keep track of all events
- A trail of the financial transactions

Usually, the applications that benefit from Event Sourcing, despite all that complexity, are a special kind of system. Those for which it is essential to keep track of the events that led to a particular state. For example, pretty much everything in the finance tech area would benefit from Event Sourcing. In such systems, you must provide an audit log, a trail of all the financial transactions, and so treating domain events as the first-class citizens makes a lot of sense here. So, CQRS can be applied on its own with great success, independently from Event Sourcing.

- CQRS
  - Doesn't require Event Sourcing
- Event Sourcing
  - Requires CQRS
- Event Sourcing without CQRS is a less scalable solution

These two concepts are mostly orthogonal to each other, mostly, but not completely. You don't need Event Sourcing to implement CQRS, but you do usually need CQRS to implement Event Sourcing. Event Sourcing without CQRS, without separating reads and writes, is a less common and less scalable solution. In theory, you could do that, but I've yet to see it being implemented in practice.

Evolutionary Design

We've discussed the evolutionary approach previously in the course, but let's reiterate it once again as it's quite an important concept.

- **You don't have to implement all the techniques from this course**
- **Defer these decisions until you have proven their need**

You don't have to implement all the techniques from this course. Do not just throw every related CQRS concept at your application. Defer these decisions until you have proven their need. And by the way, that's the approach I recommend you take with any design pattern, not just CQRS.

- **Ensure the benefits outweigh the costs before applying a pattern**

Remember, every design pattern has both costs and benefits attached to it, and you need to be sure that the benefits outweigh the costs before applying that pattern. Again, you don't need to apply all the techniques at once.

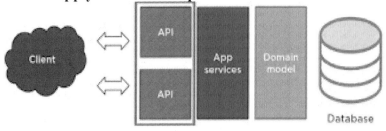

Even with just the separation at the API level, with the task-based API alone, which we implemented first in this course, you will reap significant benefits. Note that CQRS is not an application-wide pattern, like the Microservices architecture. Rather, it should be bound to a specific bounded context or microservice. It means that you can make different decisions in different bounded contexts when it comes to CQRS. Say, implement the full separation down to the data level in one bounded context, because it is very important to the business, and has high performance requirements. And at the same time, implement just the separation at the API level in another, not that important bounded context; or even keep spaghetti code with giant CRUD-oriented endpoints. That could be an option, too, depending on your project's circumstances. However, in the vast majority of enterprise-level applications, the sweet spot is the separation down to the domain model level. The separation of everything, except the database. That usually allows you to achieve the best balance between the costs and the benefits.

Using Commands and Queries from Handlers

- **Can you use other commands and queries from command and query handlers?**

There is another question that we discussed throughout this course and which merits reiteration, and that is, can you use other commands and queries from your command and query handlers? The short answer is, no, but the long answer actually differs, depending on the situation.

	Command	Query
Command handler	?	
Query handler		

There are quite a few of permutations in this question, so let's tackle them one by one. First, can you use another command from a command handler? Here is the example I brought up in an earlier module, with disenrolling the student from the existing courses before unregistering them.

```
class UnregisterCommandHandler
implements ICommandHandler{
    @Autowired
    private SessionFactory sessionFactory;
    @Autowired
    private Gate gate;
    public
UnregisterCommandHandler(SessionFactory
sessionFactory){
        sessionFactory = sessionFactory;
    }
    public Result
handle(UnregisterCommand command){
        UnitOfWork unitOfWork = new
UnitOfWork(sessionFactory);
        Repository repository = new
StudentRepository(unitOfWork);
        Student student =
repository.getById(command.Id);
        if (student == null)
            return Result.fail($"No student
found for Id {command.Id}");
        gate.dispatch(new
DisenrollCommand(student.getId(), 0,
"Unregistering"));        gate.dispatch(new
DisenrollCommand(student.getId(), 1,
"Unregistering"));
        repository.delete(student);
unitOfWork.commit();        return
Result.Ok();
    }
}
```

- Our application shouldn't trigger
  commands

You can see we are instantiating two disenroll commands, and dispatching them using the message dispatcher. It's tempting to do that, but it is contrary to the very notion of commands. It is the client that trigger commands, not our system. Our system reacts to those commands and produces domain events. It cannot create subsequent commands on its own. If you need to reuse some code between command handlers, extract it into a separate class, such as a domain service. Don't reuse command handlers themselves.

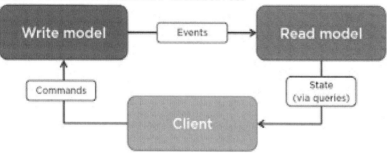

- Command: what can be done with application
- Event: what has happened to the application
- State: sum of all the events

Here's a picture that will help clarify the relationships between our application, the client, and the types of messages they exchange with each other. As you can see, the client sees the current state of the application and produces a command. The Write model receives the command and produces events. The other side of our application, the Read side, receives those events and uses them to build up the snapshot of the current state. That state is what is then shown to the client. This is the circulation of the messages and the state in the application ecosystem. A command is a representation of what the clients can do with the application, and only the client can raise them. An event is a representation of what has happened to the application. And finally, the state is the sum of all the events we've had up to this moment.

	Command	Query
Command handler	✕ Nope	？
Query handler		

Next, can you use a query from a command handler?

- Do you have a reliable way to request the current state in the command side?
- Query the command database directly
- Use a query from a command handler

Here, the answer depends on whether or not you can have a reliable way to request the current state in the command side. If you do, then no need to use a query, just refer to the command database directly to retrieve the piece of data the command needs. If there is no reliable way to request the current state, then you don't have any choice other than using a query from a command handler.

Event Sourcing

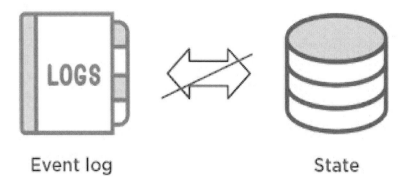

Event log   State

- Have to use the read database
- Whole set of issues related to consistency

For example, if you have implemented Event Sourcing, then the commands cannot request the current state from its own database with a reasonable performance, because rebuilding that state out of events every time you need to know something is not practical. So, you need to use the Read database, and you need to do that via a query. Note that in this case, there is a whole set of issues that come into play, because the Read and the Write databases are not immediately consistent. For example, unique constraint validations might not be done because of that. Note that they only come into play, if you are implementing Event Sourcing, and that's a story for another day.

	Command	Query
Command handler	✖ Nope	✖ Only with Event Sourcing
Query handler	✖ Nope	❓

Finally, can you use a command or a query from a query handler? Well, the answer for commands is obviously, no, because a query handler cannot mutate state. As for the use of another query from a query handler, the guidelines here are not as strict, because the Read model is immutable, and it's hard to mess up with it, thanks to this fact. But in general, I would say don't reuse the query handlers, either. Extract the common code out to some service, and use that service instead.

One-way Commands

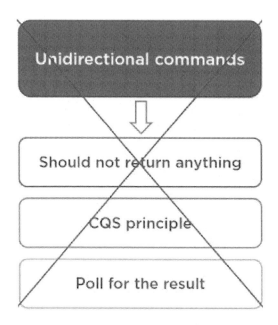

Another commonly held belief is that commands should always be unidirectional. In other words, that the commands should not return anything, because that would violate the underlying CQS principle, the Command-Query Separation Principle. The approach that is suggested instead is to poll an external source for the command execution result. So, when you, say, register a student, the command side shouldn't do that right away; it shouldn't provide you with a result synchronously, but rather it should start executing the request asynchronously, and you need to poll a separate API endpoint to know the results. That is another misconception.

- Truly one-way commands are impossible

  - Why return a locator?
  - Complete the operation synchronously
  - An Id is fine too

Truly one-way commands are impossible; they always need to return some kind of acknowledgment; either an OK, an error, or a locator, which you can use to poll the results from a separate API endpoint. And so, why return this locator if you can just return the results right away? If the operation is not inherently asynchronous, and doesn't take much time to complete, complete it synchronously, and return an OK or a validation error. If it is an update of some entity, you can also return the aggregate's new version number. No reason to implement an overcomplicated flow of events where a simple synchronous execution would do just fine. It's also fine to return an id of the newly created entity. This one looks like a true violation of the CQS principle. After all, it looks like the command returns a genuine piece of data here, but no, it's not that. It's okay for commands to return a locator of the resources they create, and if you are creating the resource synchronously, then the id of that resource would be this locator.

CQRS vs. the Specification Pattern

Alright, this is a big one. There is a controversy between two Domain-Driven Design patterns, CQRS and the Specification pattern.

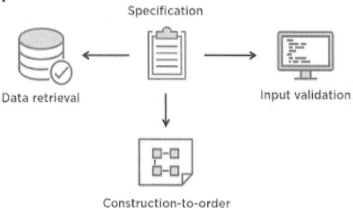

So the controversy between them is that these two patterns are incompatible. The Specification pattern allows us to encapsulate a piece of domain knowledge into a single place, and then reuse it in three scenarios; data retrieval, user input validation, and creation of a new object.

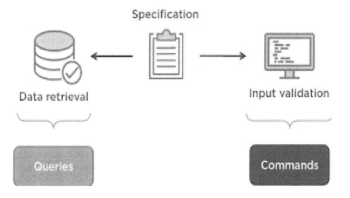

Specification

Data retrieval

Input validation

Queries

Commands

We are currently interested in only two of these three scenarios. This is useful because it allows you to avoid the domain knowledge duplication. The same domain class here would be used for both validation of the incoming data and filtration of the data in the database before showing it to the user. At the same time, the CQRS pattern proposes the separation of the two. Validation belongs to the command side, because it precedes data mutation. You validate data before you change something. Whereas data retrieval belongs to the Read side; it's what the client queries to see what data there is in our system. And so there is a clear contradiction here.

- CQRS

  - Separate domain model
  - Loose coupling

- Specifications

  - Single domain model

- The DRY principle

- Domain knowledge duplication is a lesser evil
- High coupling puts too many restrictions

On the one hand, the Specification pattern advocates for having a single domain model for these two concerns. On the other, CQRS advocates for splitting the domain model into two, and dealing with those concerns separately. So, which one is that? That's a classic example of the contradiction between the DRY principle, which stands for Don't Repeat Yourself, and the principle of loose coupling, and the guideline here is this. The loose coupling wins in the vast majority of cases, except for the simplest ones. Domain knowledge duplication is a lesser evil than the high coupling between the system components. When you duplicate the domain knowledge, it's not very convenient, but it's not that bad when you compare it to the alternative. With the high coupling, you are not able to do anything, because your hands are tied by the restrictions posed to another component. And you saw this in our sample project, too. Before we removed the domain model from the Read side, we just couldn't implement an efficient querying mechanism, all because of the unified model for commands and queries. The Specification pattern works well in simpler cases. However, in large systems, you almost always would prefer loose coupling over preventing the domain knowledge duplication between the reads and writes.

Book Summary

- CQRS pattern: what it is and how to implement it in practice
- Goals of CQRS:

  - Simplicity, performance, and scalability

- Gradually introduced the separation

  - API endpoints
  - Explicit commands, queries, and handlers, decorators
  - No domain model in reads
  - Separate database

- Synchronization between the read and write databases
- CQRS best practices and common misconceptions

We've made great progress in this book. You have learned about the CQRS pattern and how to apply it in practice. The three goals of CQRS are simplicity, performance, and scalability; simplicity being the most important one. We gradually introduced more and more separation to our system. First, we separated our API endpoints, and split the single giant update method into several task-based ones. That allowed us to transition away from the CRUD-based thinking, and introduce a task-based interface, both the UI and the API. Next, we extracted explicit commands and queries, and handlers for them out of our controller. That allowed us to introduce a unified interface for the handlers, and then create decorators to tackle cross-cutting concerns with the minimal amount of effort. After that, we extracted the domain model out of the Read side, which allowed us to both simplify the domain model and write high-performance SQL queries for the Read side. Next, we introduced the separation at the data level. We created a separate database for reads with the schema perfectly aligned with the needs of the Read model. That allowed us to improve the performance, simplify the Read model even further, and enable scalability on the query side. Finally, we discussed the synchronization between the Read and Write databases, and we also discussed best practices and common misconceptions around the CQRS pattern.

29293743R00115

Made in the USA
San Bernardino, CA
13 March 2019